SAVED,

MADE FREE

and

DELIVERED

Carmen Y. Woods

ISBN 978-1-63630-153-2 (Paperback)
ISBN 978-1-63630-154-9 (Digital)

Covenant Books, Inc.
11661 Hwy 707
Murrells Inlet, SC 29576
www.covenantbooks.com

To my husband, Charles, our bloodlines (families) and the entire body of Christ. My desire is that you walk in the freedom and victory Jesus purchased with his blood on Calvary (Acts 20:8, 1 Corinthians 6:19–20).

Foreword

Carmen and I have been married for twenty-eight years. In that time, I have seen her grow into a kind, compassionate, and loving woman of God. She has a heart for God's people. Here lies the reason for this book.

Now take the words of this book, read them, devour them, digest them, but most of all, do them. "But be ye doers of the word, and not hearers only, deceiving your own selves" (James 1:22).

This book was written for such a time as this.

Enjoy and God bless you all,
Elder Charles O. Woods Sr.

Introduction

The devil, the enemy of your soul, is a mind blinder, a deceiver, and a liar. The Bible says in Matthew 13:28, "An enemy has done this." He has sown tares in the field with the wheat. The enemy wants to keep God's people blinded, confused, and living defeated lives. He has put thoughts in your mind and have you thinking and saying things as if they are your thoughts.

Jesus says, "He come that you might have life, and that you may have it more abundantly" (John 10:10). Abundant in love, abundant in mercy, abundant in forgiveness, abundant in caring, abundant in healing, abundant in him. He has given us the keys to the kingdom. He said in his Word, "Whatever you bind on earth shall be bound in heaven and whatever you loose on earth shall be loosed in heaven" (Matthew 16:19, Matthew 18:18).

Jesus came to set you free from the tricks, schemes, and plans of the enemy. God sent his son, Jesus, born of a virgin, to redeem us back to him. Let's walk in the victory, love, and power that Jesus purchased with his blood. Let's live the life God planned for us.

"Whom the Son has made free, is free indeed" (John 8:36).

Week 1

Brethren, I count not myself to have apprehended: but this one thing I do, forgetting those things which are behind, and reaching forth unto those things which are before. I press toward the mark for the prize of the high calling of God in Christ Jesus.
—Philippians 3:13–14

As we are in the New Year, don't bring into the New Year those things that hold you back, keep you down, keep you bound, sorrowful, and depressed. Shed them off. We are only to look back on where God has brought us from. How he has delivered us from situations and give him praise. Use the deliverance of past victories to propel you forward into your destiny, not draw you back into that place and time. We are to look back and say, "Lord, you did that for me, I know you can do this." Don't dwell on the past. Put your focus and faith in Jesus. You are walking into a new season.

"Stop looking back, you're not going that way" (Author unknown).

Read: *Luke 9:62, 2 Corinthians 5:17, Romans 8:37, 1 John 4:4, Jeremiah 31:34, Hebrews 8:12, Philippians 4:13, Isaiah 43:18–19, Isaiah 43:25, Isaiah 44:22.*

Week 2

That if thou shalt confess with thy mouth the Lord Jesus, and shalt believe in thine heart that God hath raised him from the dead, thou shalt be saved. For with the heart man believeth unto righteousness; and with the mouth confession is made unto salvation.

—Romans 10:9–10

Confess with your mouth, believe in your heart, and you will be saved. Confess Jesus as Lord and Savior of your life. Confess your sins to Jesus and ask him to forgive you of them. Repent and turn to God. Repent means to turn away from. Don't turn 360 degrees, you will just turn in a circle and end up where you started but turn 180 degrees to God. Start walking toward him and away from sin. He is there waiting for you. Let Jesus rule your heart. Let him lead and guide you on which way to go, which way not to go, what to say, or what not to say. There may be times when you may have to stand still and not do a thing. In Exodus 14:13, Moses told the people to "fear ye not, stand still and see the salvation of the Lord." There are going to be times when you just have to stand still and let the Lord fight your battles. "The battle is not yours, but Gods" (2 Chronicles 20:15).

The Bible says, "Neither is there salvation in any other; for there is none other name under heaven given among men, whereby we must be saved" (Acts 4:12). Jesus said, "No man cometh unto the Father, but by me" (John 14:6). There is no other way, no other person who can get you to heaven but Jesus. We need a relationship with the Father through his son, Jesus.

Things may not be easy. Just because you are saved does not mean all your problems will disappear or that you will live a carefree life. God wants to get the glory out of your life. So when you are going through difficult times just look to Jesus, he is where your help comes from (Hebrews 12:2, Psalm 121:1–3). Jesus said that he would never leave you nor forsake you (Hebrews 13:5–6). He said he would be with you even until the end of the world (Matthew 28:20). Whatever problems you face, Jesus is right there with you. Going through with you, just like he did for Daniel in the lion's den (Daniel 6:16–22) and for Shadrach, Meshach, and Abednego in the fiery furnace (Daniel 3:8–30). Know that God loves you, and he would never put more on you than you can bear (1 Corinthians 10:13). He will deliver you.

As you live for Christ, people you used to hang around, you won't want to hang around them anymore. Places you used to go, you won't want to go there anymore. Things you used to do, you won't want to do them anymore. As Christ fills your life, you will become different and see things differently like God does. Not because you are better than anyone but because you are different. You have given your life to Christ, and you want to live for him. You won't be lonely or alone because God will replace those old friends and give you new ones, ones who are living for him. He has so many wonderful blessings for you.

Let the Lord know that you want to live for him not for Satan. He is the one who came to die for your sins (John 1:29). Every sin that you have committed, the sins you commit daily, and the sins you will commit in the future. You may say, I am not going to sin. But the truth of the matter is we live in this world fighting against an enemy (the devil) who is fighting against us. The Bible says, "For all have sinned and fallen short of the glory of God" (Romans 3:23). "If you say you have not sinned, you make him a liar, and the truth is not in you" (1 John 1:10). You may not intend to sin or may not even be aware that you have sinned.

Accept Jesus as your personal Lord and Savior. He loves you, and he wants to make you free (John 8:36), free from the law of sin, free from sin and shame, and free from the enemy who is trying to keep you bound. Jesus said that he came that we might have life, and we might have it more abundantly (John 10:10).

"Submit yourself to God, resist the devil and he will flee from you" (James 4:7).

Read: *Exodus 14:13, 2 Chronicles 20:15, Acts 4:12, John 14:6, Hebrews 12:2, Psalm 121:1–3, Hebrews 13:5–6, Matthew 28:20, Daniel 6:16–22; Daniel 3:8–30, 1 Corinthians 10:13, John 1:29, Romans 3:23, 1 John 1:10, John 10:10.*

Week 3

Jesus answered and said, Verily, verily, I say unto thee, except a man
be born again, he cannot see the kingdom of God. Verily, Verily,
I say unto thee, except a man be born of water and of the Spirit,
he cannot enter into the kingdom of God. That which is born of
the flesh is flesh; and that which is born of the Spirit is spirit.
—John 3:3, 5–6

When you are born, you are physically born in the flesh. And
thus being in the flesh, you do things of the flesh—fornication, idol-
atry, hatred, lie, cheat, steal, etc. (Galatians 5:19–21). The fleshly
man can neither see nor enter into the kingdom of God because he is
blind to spiritual truth. "He can neither obey, understand nor please
God" (The Scofield Study Bible Commentary 2003). Because of the
sin of Adam and Eve in the Garden of Eden, we are all born into sin
(Read Genesis 3). You were born of the flesh, but you must be born
of the spirit.

Being born of the water is a cleansing from an old self (life in
the flesh) to a new self (life in the spirit). When you are born again,
when you accept Jesus Christ as your Lord and Savior, God sends
his spirit, the Holy Spirit, to dwell in you. As God's spirit dwells in
you, the old nature will die. The Holy Spirit will begin to teach you
all truths and show you things to come (John 16:13, 1 Corinthians
2:9–12, Ephesians 3:5).

As you grow in Christ and learn the truth of the Word of God,
the devil will have no more hold on you. Nothing he says or does will
matter because you will now know the truth, and you will be free.
The Word of God says, "If the Son therefore, shall make you free, ye
shall be free indeed" (John 8:36). You will be free to worship, free to

pray, free to bring your cares and concerns to God, and free to exercise your faith in God and in his word.

Read: *Galatians 5:19–21, 1 Corinthians 2:14, Romans 8:8, Jeremiah 17:9, Mark 7:21–23, Genesis 3, John 16:13, 1 Corinthians 2:9–12, Ephesians 3:5.*

Week 4

Pour out your heart before him.

—Psalm 62:8

The him this scripture is talking about is God. He is concerned with what concerns you. There is nothing you may go through in your life that God is not concerned about. No matter how small or insignificant you think it may be, if it concerns you, then it concerns God. During your prayer time, just tell him what is on your mind, what is in your heart, what you are going through, and what you like and don't like. Share your praises with him and thank him for his grace and mercy. Sure, he already knows, but he wants you to come to him, for you to take the time to talk with him. He delights in his people.

Once you tell God what is on your heart and you need help, just ask him. Let him know that you want him to have his way in your life. Ask him to show you how to move in the situation. Let him know that you want to surrender all to him. All means everything, not just some things, not things you think you can take care of, not things you think he doesn't want to hear or are insignificant. Surrender all. God will answer. There may be times when you have to be still (Psalm 46:10) and wait on God (Isaiah 40:31). If this is God's answer, then be still and wait. Believe me, the wait will be worth it, no matter how long.

In 1 Samuel 1:15, Hannah poured out her heart before God. She wanted to have a son, and he granted her request. In Genesis 18:10–14 and Genesis 21:1–5, God granted Abraham and Sarah a son after they were both past child bearing age. Is there anything too hard for God (Jeremiah 32:27)? I say there is nothing too hard for God. Nothing he will not do for his people (Luke 11:13).

God wants you to surrender your life to him, all of your cares, all of your concerns, everything to him.

Read: *Psalm 46:10, Isaiah 40:31, 1 Samuel 1:15, Genesis 18:10–14, Genesis 21:1–5, Jeremiah 32:27, Luke 11:13.*

Week 5

For verily I say unto you, That whosoever shall say unto this
mountain, Be thou removed, and be thou cast into the sea; and
shall not doubt in his heart, but shall believe that those things
which he saith shall come to pass; he shall have whatsoever he saith.
—Mark 11:23.

W hat you say has power and is important in the kingdom of God.
In Genesis 1, God spoke the world into existence. When he spoke it,
it happened. The foundation of the earth was made. The same thing
happens with you. Depending on what you say, you either do it or
don't do it. You do what you say you are going to do or you don't do
what you say you are not going to do. Either way, you do what you
say.

What you say can be used to build a person up or tear them
down. Once you say something, you can't pull it back. It is in the
atmosphere. So be careful what you say.

What someone says can have a lasting effect in your life and
can determine your destiny, whether good or bad. You can probably
think back in your life of something someone said to you when you
were a child, and you still remember it. Someone may have said something negative to you, and Satan keeps reminding you of it. If that
is happening, I encourage you to get before God and cast it down.
Rebuke it from your mind and your thoughts. Confess 2 Corinthians
10:4–5. Continue to confess the scripture until it departs your mind.
There is a saying, "Sticks and stones may break my bones, but words
will never hurt me." That is a lie straight from hell. There are many
people walking around today bound up by something someone said
to them when they were a child.

If you are in a relationship with someone or has friends who are constantly saying negative things to you, about you, or others, then you need to let them go out of your life, no matter how long you have been friends. Seek God, and he will give you instructions. Remember God is not trying to bring you down or leave you alone; he is trying to get you to him.

On the other hand, someone may have said something encouraging that lifted you. Something that made you feel good about yourself and your life. Something that made you feel like you mattered and had worth. Something that made you feel as if you could do anything. Something that propelled you forward into your destiny.

I encourage you to confess only God's words over yourself and others. Train yourself to say what God has said about you and about others. Don't say negative things. Say what God has said. And when you say what God has said, believe it. Don't just say it. Believe that what He has said will come to pass, and you shall have whatsoever you say (Mark 11:23).

"Death and life are in the power of the tongue: and they that love it shall eat the fruit thereof" (Proverbs 18:21).

Read: *Genesis 1, 2 Corinthians 10:4–5, Matthew 18:19, Matthew 21:22, Mark 11:24, John 14:13, John 15:7, Proverbs 18:21, Proverbs 3:5–6.*

Week 6

As far as the east is from the west, so far hath
he removed our transgressions from us.

—Psalm 103:12

M*erriam-Webster* defines transgression as a "violation of a law, command or duty" (Merriam-Webster 2019). Any transgression of God's law, knowingly or unknowingly, is a sin.

Once God reveals to you the sin in your life, acknowledge it to him then ask him to forgive you no matter how long ago it happened. Don't try to hide, lie, or make excuses. If he reveals it, confess it, repent, and ask for forgiveness. Then walk in that forgiveness and don't let anyone convince you otherwise. Pray the prayer that David prayed in Psalm 51. Pray it from the heart because true repentance comes from the heart. Remember the Bible says that "out of the abundance of the heart the mouth speaketh" (Matthew 12:34, Luke 6:45). God is not listening to your mouth; he is listening to your heart (1 Samuel 16:7).

God does not want that anyone should die and go to hell. When he removes your sins, he forgives them. He throws them into the sea of forgetfulness. He does not remember them anymore (Hebrews 10:17). They are blotted out of your life. Isaiah 43:25 says, "I, even I, am he that blotteth out thy transgressions for mine own sake, and will not remember thy sins." They are forgotten.

So when the enemy tries to throw you a pity party and have you feeling bad and worthless about all the things you have done wrong just remind him of God's word in Psalm 103:12.

God is faithful; he holds true to his word.

Have faith and believe the Word of God. He will do just what he said he will do (Isaiah 55:11).

Read: *Isaiah 38:17, Isaiah 44:22, Acts 3:19, 1 John 1:9.*

Week 7

Therefore if any man be in Christ, he is a new creature; old
things are passed away; behold all things are become new.
—2 Corinthians 5:17

W hen you accept Jesus as your personal Lord and Savior, he will
begin to change your life. You will become a new creature in him.
No longer will you be held bound by your past sins. All the ungodly
things in the past that you used to do, you won't want to do them
anymore. They will gradually pass away.

To be in Christ means that you walk and live in Christ day
by day. That you do not "walk after the flesh, but after the Spirit"
(Romans 8:1, 4). You "deny ungodliness and worldly lusts, and live
soberly, righteously, and godly, in this present world" (Titus 2:12).
It means that you bear the fruit of the spirit (Galatians 5:22–23),
and you abide in Christ (John 15:4). You become "as connected
and attached to Christ as members of the body are connected and
attached to each other" (1 Corinthians 12:12–27) and "as the branch
is connected and attached to the vine" (John 15:4–7, Preacher's
Outline and Sermon Bible-Commentary, Wordsearch 12).

Jesus paid the price for us to be free. He paid the price for us
to be changed, to become new creatures. When you have spent time
with Jesus, you can't help but to be changed. When Jesus encountered
people on his way to the cross, they were all changed (Read Matthew
9:20–22, Mark 10:52, Luke 8:26–39, John 4:1–25, Matthew 15:30).
Old things had passed away, they became new.

The Lord gave me the below poem on Tuesday, April 11, 2017,
around five thirty during my morning time with him.

Your blood, it cleans, it washes me white as snow.
Your blood, it cleans me from head to toe.

Just think about snow. When you wake up in the morning and look at it before anyone goes outside to mess with it, it is a blanket of pure, sparking white. Just imagine Jesus's blood pouring on you from your head to your toe. As it runs down your body, you are cleansed. All the sins, negativity, wrong thoughts, hurts, pains, sickness, and ugliness are all washed away. You are forgiven. You are free. You are white as snow. Jesus was letting me know that his blood had cleansed me and made me white as snow. He can do the same for you.

So when people try to remind you of your past and what you used to do, just remind them of 2 Corinthians 5:17.

Read: *Matthew 8, Mark 7, Luke 8.*

Week 8

Then came Peter to him, and said, Lord, how oft shall
my brother sin against me, and I forgive him? till seven
times? Jesus saith unto him, I say not unto thee, Until
seven times: but, Until seventy times seven.

—Matthew 18:21–22

In this scripture, Jesus is not saying to forgive your brother 490 times. He is saying to forgive him as many times as it takes. God has forgiven us endlessly, way past seventy times seven.

Can you imagine keeping track of the number of times you forgive someone? You would have to keep a log of each person you forgave. And what if you lost track of how many times you had forgiven them, then what? I forgave Mary 100 times, Paul 250 times, Susan 300 times, and Elizabeth 50 times. I have only one more to go for Thomas, and he will have been forgiven 490 times. After that, that's it. So what happens when you need to forgive Thomas after 490 times? What if God kept track and only forgave us 490 times? Lord, I would have been dead and gone a long time ago.

No, Jesus is saying to forgive your brother endlessly. As often as he sins against you, you should forgive him, not keep track or keep count of how many times you have already forgiven him. The Word of God says in Matthew 6:14–15, "For if ye forgive men their trespasses, your heavenly Father will also forgive you: But if ye forgive not men their trespasses, neither will your Father forgive your trespasses." In order to be forgiven, you have to forgive. The Bible says with the same measure, you "mete it shall be measured to you again" (Matthew 7:2). In other words, if you won't forgive your brother or sister because he said something about you, your heavenly Father will not forgive you when you say something about someone else, no matter how small or insignificant you think it may be.

You may have read this in Luke 6:38, "Give, and it shall be given unto you; good measure, pressed down, and shaken together, and running over. For with the same measure that ye mete withal it shall be measured to you again." I say forgive, and it shall be forgiven of you with good measure, pressed down, shaken together, and running over will God forgive you.

Read: *Isaiah 43:24, Jeremiah 31:34, Micah 7:18–20, Mark 11:25–26, Acts 10:42–43, James 5:15–16, Luke 6:38.*

Week 9

Learn to do well.

—Isaiah 1:17

Learn to do well. Let the Lord teach you how to do well, how to worship him, how to praise him, and how to do what the scriptures say. As you seek God daily and keep your mind stayed on him, he will help you to think on things that are true, things that are honest, things that are just, things that are pure, things that are lovely, and things that are a good report (Philippians 4:8). As you trust God and fill your life with his word, he will push out the old stuff, the old you.

Ask God to teach you to trust him with everything in your life. How do you do this you may ask? By saying what God has said and then believing that his word will come to pass in your life. Mark 11:24 says, "Therefore I say unto you, what things soever ye desire, when ye pray, believe that ye receive them, and ye shall have them." God's word is active and alive today. It will do today what it did yesterday. The same God that delivered his people from Egypt is the same God we serve to day. The same miracles he did when Jesus walked the earth, he is doing them today. You just have to believe and trust the Lord.

Learn the scriptures. Confess them over your life. Confess them over the lives of your children. Believe the Word of God. Ask the Lord to help you. Ask him to order your steps every day (Psalm 119:133). Believe God that wherever you are is where he needs you to be. Prosper and grow where he has planted you. Be a blessing to the people around you. Let them see God in your life.

And when the enemy tries to move and cause havoc in your thinking, and he will, just rebuke him and confess 2 Corinthians 10:4–5. Keep your heart always to God. Always seeking him. Always trusting him. Always praising him. Always thanking him. Always learning of him. Purpose in your heart to learn of God. Purpose in your heart to follow God. Love the things that he loves and hate the things that he hates.

Learn not to talk about people. Learn not to judge people. Learn not to think negatively.

Read: *Psalm 27:1–5, Psalm 28:7–9, Psalm 31, Psalm 34:1–4,8,19, Psalm 37:1–7.*

Week 10

Delight thyself also in the Lord; and he shall
give thee the desires of thine heart.

—Psalm 37:4

W hen you desire to please the Lord and surrender your life to
him, then your desire becomes his desire. Whatever the Lord wants
to do with you, it is okay with you because you want to please him. It
doesn't matter where he wants to send you. It doesn't matter what he
wants you to do. It doesn't even matter what he tells you to say. You
will do or say it because it is the desire of the Lord.

The Believers Bible Commentary gives this example,

> But suppose you have had great desires to
> carry on a certain ministry for the Lord. You feel
> confident that he has been leading you, and your
> only desire is to glorify him. Yet a powerful adver-
> sary has opposed, blocked, and thwarted you at
> every bend in the road. What do you do in a case
> like this? The answer is that you delight yourself
> also in the Lord, knowing that in his own time
> he shall give you the desires of your heart. It is
> not necessary for you to fight back. "The battle
> is not yours, but God's" (2 Chronicles 20:15).
> "The Lord will fight for you, and you shall hold
> your peace" (Exodus 14:14). (Believer's Bible
> Commentary: A Thorough, Yet Easy-to-Read
> Bible Commentary That Turns Complicated
> Theology into Practical Understanding)

Give the Lord praise, honor, and glory because he is going to work things out for his glory.

The Lord will do whatever is necessary to bring your desire to pass. He will provide the place, people, and resources for you to carry on the ministry. You must be careful to wait on the Lord and not take matters into your own hand. He has it, and he is in control. Your heart, mind, and soul are intertwined with the Lord. Your desire will become his desire, and his desire will become your desire. You will only want what he wants.

Don't get jealous or weary in doing good for the Lord because the unsaved or wicked seem to be prospering. You may be making little strides and sometimes even staying where you are. Believe me, you *will* get your reward. The Word of God says, "And let us not be weary in well doing: for in due season we shall reap, if we faint not" (Galatians 6:9). God's word also says, "Fret not thyself because of evildoers, neither be thou envious against the workers of iniquity. For they shall soon be cut down like the grass and wither as the green herb" (Psalm 37:1–2).

I encourage you to keep your focus on the Lord and desire him and his ways with all your heart above all else.

Read: *Isaiah 58:14, Psalm 145:19–20, Matthew 7:7–8, Psalm 90:5–6.*

Week 11

There is therefore now no condemnation to them which are in Christ Jesus, who walk not after the flesh, but after the Spirit.

—Romans 8:1

Condemnation is not from God; it is from the enemy. The enemy uses condemnation to get and keep you bound. Condemnation will have you blaming yourself and not forgiving yourself. The enemy condemns you to keep you feeling sad, depressed, down, and gloomy. To keep you preoccupied with *You*. What *You* have done wrong. What *You* want. Continually telling *You*, *You* don't please God. *You* are no good. God will never forgive *You*. God doesn't love *You*.

The Word of God says in Revelations 12:10 that "the accuser of our brethren (the devil) is cast down, which accused them before God day and night." He is constantly before the Father accusing you. Reminding him of what you did wrong, what you said about this person, the bad thoughts you had. But you see Jesus is there too, saying to the Father, I died for that. My blood paid the price for that. There is nothing the enemy can bring against you that Jesus has not already paid for. Your life is bought and paid in full.

Once you confess Jesus as your Lord and Savior, you are free from condemnation. The enemy no longer has any hold on you. You must purpose in your heart to "walk not after the flesh but after the Spirit" (Romans 8:1).

Purpose in your heart to follow after Jesus. Turn from the old you unto the new you. Read scriptures daily. Pray often. Rise early to spend time in prayer with the Lord. Listen and sing songs of praise and worship that glorify God and not the flesh. Songs that lift him up. The Word says, "And I, if I be lifted up from the earth, will draw all men unto me" (John 12:32). When the enemy comes against you cast him down immediately. Give him no place (Ephesians 4:27).

Thank God for Jesus Christ!!!

Read: *Galatians 5:22–25, Hebrews 12:2, 2 Corinthians 10:4–5, Philippians 1:6.*

Week 12

For the word of God is quick, and powerful, and sharper
than any twoedged sword, piercing even to the dividing
asunder of soul and spirit, and of the joints and marrow, and
is a discerner of the thoughts and intents of the heart.
—Hebrews 4:12

"The "word of God" is that which God speaks-whether it
be a promise or a threatening; whether it be law or gospel;
whether it be a simple declaration or a statement of a doctrine.
The idea here is, that what God had said is fitted to detect
hypocrisy, and to lay open the true nature of the feelings of the
soul, so that there can be no escape for the guilty. His truth is
adapted to bring out the real feelings, and to show man exactly
what he is. Truth always has this power-whether preached,
or read, or communicated by conversation, or impressed
upon the memory and conscience by the Holy Spirit."
(Barnes' Notes on the New Testament)

The Word of God is sharp. It cuts going in, and it cuts coming out.
Penetrating "to the deepest and most inward and secret parts of the
heart, wounding them deadly that are stubborn, and plainly quick-
ening the believers" (The 1599 Geneva Bible).

"The truth of God is all-penetrating and searching, and that the
real thoughts and intents of the heart will be brought to light; and
that if there is insincerity and self-deception, there can be no hope
of escape" (Barnes' Notes on the New Testament). The Word of God
will reveal what is in the heart and it is the heart that matters. It is the
heart that God looks at (1 Samuel 16:7).

As you read the Word, all of the things you are doing that is not pleasing to the Lord should produce conviction. Once you are convicted, you should repent, ask God for forgiveness, and then ask him for *help*! Help in the name of Jesus (John 14:13–14). Whatever help you need, help to stop, help to start, help to forgive, help to keep you focused on him, or help to move all of the distractions out of the way.

So as you read the Word of God, surrender all to him. Don't hide anything from him. Let him heal you. Let him wash away all your sins and give you true forgiveness. As you surrender your life to the Lord, he will slowly cut out those things that you confess to him and ask for help. He will heal the wound that was caused by the cut as only he can. He will never leave you alone (Matthew 28:20).

Read: *Romans 10:9–10, Psalm 121, Psalm 62:8, Psalm 103:12, Hebrews 12:1–2, Ephesians 6:10–18, Psalm 139:23–24.*

Week 13

Search me, O God, and know my heart; try me, and know
my thoughts: and see if there be any wicked way in me, and
lead me in the way everlasting. ...cleanse thou me from secret
faults. Keep back thy servant also from presumptuous sins; let
them not have dominion over me: then shall I be upright, and
I shall be innocent from the great transgression. Let the words
of my mouth, and the meditation of my heart, be acceptable
in thy sight, O Lord, my strength, and my redeemer.
—Psalm 139:23–24, Psalm 19:12–14

These scriptures are often quoted together, thereby leaving you to
think they are one scripture when they are, in fact, a few scriptures in
different chapters of Psalm.

During your prayer time as you are in worship with the Lord,
as you pray these scriptures, the Lord will slowly begin to cleanse
your heart and mind (1 John 1:9). As the Lord brings things to
your remembrance, don't deny them no matter how big or small.
Acknowledge what you have done, then repent, and ask God for
forgiveness. Ask the Lord to order your steps (Psalm 119:133) to lead
you in the way you should go (Psalm 32:8).

As you seek to draw closer to God, ask him to search your heart
and remove anything that is there that is keeping you from him. Ask
him to cleanse any secrets you may have. You may be able to keep
secrets from your family and friends but not from God. He knows
what's in your heart. So ask him to cleanse you from secrets you
attempt to keep from him. Confess it, ask forgiveness, forgive yourself, and live free. Believe me, you will be blessed and glad you did.

Presumptuous sins are things that you presume are sins. You're
not sure, but in your mind, they are sins. Ask the Lord to keep you

from those things and give you complete clarity in knowing. You don't need anything holding you captive or keeping you in bondage. There is freedom in Jesus. You don't need to be bound by presuming something you said or did is a sin. Jesus came to make you free (John 8:36).

As you surrender to God, he will change what you say and change your heart. You will no longer say and believe what the world is saying. You will say and believe what God has said. You will no longer care what the world thinks about you, only what God thinks, and you will long to please him.

If you don't have a prayer time, I encourage you to start one. Spend time with the Lord. Praying in accordance with ACTS (adoration, confession, thanksgiving, and supplication) (Sproul 2018). There are even times during your prayer time where you may just need to put on some music, or not, and sit before God. Not saying anything, just letting him minister to you. Letting him fill you up to overflowing.

Read: *1 John 1:9, Psalm 119:133, Psalm 32:8, Galatians 5:13, Galatians 5:1, John 8:36, John 3:16.*

Week 14

I love the LORD, because he hath heard my voice and
my supplications. Because he hath inclined his ear unto
me, therefore will I call upon him as long as I live.
—Psalm 116:1–2

When you belong to the Lord, he will hear you when you call upon him. It doesn't matter what you are going through, if you call upon the name of the Lord, he will hear you and be there to help you through whatever situation you are going through. The Bible says he is a very present help in time of trouble (Psalm 46:1).

You know how it is with your children. They can be in a room full of children, but when your child says Momma or cries, you will know it is your child. You recognize your child's voice and spring into action to see what is going on. That's how it is with God. When we call upon him, he will recognize our voice and come to our aid.

This scripture really speaks to me because it is real and true in my life. So many times I have cried out unto the Lord. He heard my voice and my supplications. How do I know? Because he answered my prayers. Not always in the way and time that I wanted them answered, but he always answered them. Giving me just what I needed rather than what I wanted.

I love the Lord for his grace and his mercy in my life, for always being there listening to me when I cry out to him, for always providing answers, and for always answering prayers. I will call upon him as long as I live because I know he loves me. I know he has my best interest at heart and would never do anything to hurt me. Everything he does is for my good and his glory, even chastisement. For those he loves, he chastens (Hebrew 12:6). I am eternally grateful and in awe that God loves me so much. That he has forgiven my sins and is always waiting to hear from me.

The things that God has done for me, he can do for you. Surrender your life to him. Call on the Lord all the days of your life. He sits ready to hear your voice and answer your call.

Read: *Jeremiah 33:3, Romans 10:13, Psalm 46:1, Psalm 103:12, Hebrews 12:6.*

Week 15

I will lift up mine eyes unto the hills, from whence cometh my help. My help cometh from the LORD, which made heaven and earth.

—Psalm 121:1–3

Lift your eyes to the Lord and call upon him when you need help. It doesn't matter what kind of help you need; the Lord will help you. The Lord will never leave you nor forsake you (Deuteronomy 31:6, Hebrews 13:5). He will always be there to help. He loves you that much.

Look to the Lord for help not man. Man may let you down, but the Lord will never let you down. When everyone else has forsaken you, when no one else wants anything to do with you, when no one will answer their phone when you call, when no one will reply to your text or Facebook posts, when no one is there to hear your cries for help, just look to the Lord. He will be right there. It doesn't matter the day or hour; he is waiting for your call. No matter what the enemy may say, no matter what he may do, always call on the Lord for help. As you call on him for help, just see how he steps in and takes over, see how smoothly things go, see how he provides just the right answer at the right time—the answer you need.

The Bible says he is a very present help in times of trouble (Psalm 46:1). So when you have trouble, as we all do because we have a devil who is constantly fighting against us, look to the Lord for help, comfort, and peace.

There are times when the enemy attacks me, and I have to call upon the Lord for help. Yes, I can have my husband pray for me, but it is the Lord who answers my call. He gives me comfort and peace that only he can give. It doesn't matter what I am going through, what situation I have; I look to the Lord for help. I look to him with expectancy, knowing that He is going to answer my prayer and provide the help I need.

The Bible says in Isaiah 55:6 to "seek the Lord while he may be found, call upon him while he is near." This leads you to believe there may be a time when you call upon him, and you won't find him, and he won't be near.

Call on the Lord any day or time. He is waiting to hear from you.

Read: *Jeremiah 33:3, 2 Chronicles 14:11, Psalm 33:20, Psalm 37:40, Psalm 42:5, Psalm 124:8, Psalm 146:3, Psalm 146:5, Isaiah 41:10, 13, Isaiah 50:9.*

Week 16

In righteousness shalt thou be established: thou shalt
be far from oppression; for thou shalt not fear: and
from terror; for it shall not come near thee.

—Isaiah 54:14

Righteousness is being "in right standing with God" (Delgado 2013). When you have confessed your sins to God, I mean really confessed your sins to him, turned from them, and purpose in your heart to follow after God, he clothes you with righteousness. Not that you deserve it but because of his grace and mercy, he gives you righteousness. He sees your heart, knows your confession is true, and you desire to trust and follow him.

Oppression is defined in *Merriam-Webster* as "a sense of being weighed down in body or mind; depression." Oppression is not from God; it is from the devil. The devil's desire is to keep you oppressed and depressed, keep you feeling as if you will never be forgiven. You will never come out. You will never amount to anything. That no one loves you. That no one cares. There is no hope. The devil will tell you that you will never be as good as him or her. The devil will have you looking at someone else's life and seeing what they have and what they do and measuring your life against their life. *The devil is a liar!*

Seek the face of God. Ask for his leading and guidance in your life. There is nothing in your life that God can't handle. The place you are in right now, God knew you would be there, and he is waiting on your call for help to bring you out, to bring you up, to set your feet on a rock (Psalm 40:2). There is nothing he will not forgive. No situation too hard for the Lord (Jeremiah 32:27). Trust him to lead your life. He loves you. As a matter of fact, the reason why you are going through what you are going through is because God is calling you. Calling you out of the world and unto him (2 Corinthians 6:17–18). The Word of God says, "I stand at the door, and knock: any man hear my voice, and open the door, I will come in to him, and will sup with him, and he with me." (Revelations 3:20). Answer the call of the Lord. Let him in. Have supper with the Lord.

I come to tell you that you can be free in the name of Jesus. Jesus came to destroy the works of the devil (1 John 3:8). He came to make you free (John 8:36), to give you hope and a future (Jeremiah 29:11).

Surrender *all* to God. He is worthy.

Read: *Romans 3:25, Psalm 40:2, Jeremiah 32:27, 2 Corinthians 6:17–18, Revelations 3:20, 1 John 3:8, John 8:36, Jeremiah 29:11, 2 Corinthians 10:12.*

Week 17

The king's heart is in the hand of the Lord, as the
rivers of water: he turneth it withersoever he will.
—Proverbs 21:1

J ust like God turns the course of the rivers of water, he can turn the
heart of man. No one is in control of his own life. God is, whether
they believe it or not, whether they believe in him or not. He still
controls everything. You've heard it said, "A self-made man." He is
not self-made but God made. He succeeded in his endeavors only
because God allowed it. Jesus said, "For without me, you can do
nothing" (John 15:5).

No man can act independently of God (Thru The Bible with J.
Vernon McGee). There may be some who think they can. There are
rulers in this world who believe they have all the power, all the control, and all the money. They may have all those things, but God ulti-
mately owns it all. "The silver is mine, and the gold is mine," declares
the Lord (Haggai 2:8). "The cattle upon a thousand hills" belong to
the Lord (Psalm 50:10). He is in control and owns *everything!*

The same is true in our lives. God is in control of everything.
All those trials and tribulations you have gone through have been
allowed by God. Even when you got off track or out of his will, he
will never turn his back on you. Just like he turns the rivers (Proverbs
21:20), he is right there turning things in our lives. He said he would
never leave us nor forsake us (Deuteronomy 31:6, Hebrews 13:5),
and he meant just that.

As you surrender your heart to the Lord, give him permission
to turn it any way he pleases. Purpose to give your will to the will of
the Father, not to do what you want to do but to do what he wants
you to do. Let God get the glory out of your life. Be a testimony of

God's goodness and mercy to others. Let others see the things God has done for you. Give them hope that just like he did it for you, if they turn their lives over to him, he will do it for them.

The Bible says to "Delight thyself also in the Lord; and he shall give thee the desires of thine heart" (Psalm 37:4). Let God's desires be your desires. Let him turn your heart anyway he pleases.

Read: *John 15:5, Haggai 2:7–8, Psalm 50:12, Deuteronomy 31:6, Hebrews 13:5, Psalm 37:4, Acts 10:34, Revelation 12:11.*

Week 18

My son, attend to my words; incline thine ear unto
my sayings. Let them not depart from thine eyes; keep
them in the midst of thine heart. For they are life unto
those that find them, and health to all their flesh.

—Proverbs 4:20–22

What I hear when I read this scripture is that we need to know the Word of God. We need to know what the Father has said to us so when we hear false doctrines or the devil tries to deceive us, we will know it is a lie. We need to know God's promises to us.

If you never read that whom the Son is made free is free indeed (John 8:36), you would never walk in freedom, and you would forever be bound. If you never read that you could pour out your heart (Psalm 62:8) and confess your sins to the Lord and he would forgive your sins, you would never confess your faults to him and walk in the forgiveness he so freely gives (1 John 1:9). If you never read that God so loved you that he gave his only begotten son so that whosoever believed in him would not perish but have everlasting life (John 3:16), you would never believe on the Lord and give your life to Christ.

Beloved, make a purpose to read the scriptures daily. Set aside time to spend with the Lord reading his Word. Keep the Word of God always in your heart, always in your hearing, meditating on it, rehearsing it over and over in your mind. As you do this, it will settle in your heart. All of your doubts and fears will become faith and trust in the Lord.

Make a change in your life. When you listen to music, listen to songs that lift up the name of Jesus. Play the Bible on CD in your car. Let the Word of God fill your house and dispel any evil spirits. When you leave the house for the day, put praise and worship music on, set it to repeat and let it play and fill the atmosphere while you are gone. When you go to bed at night, put the Bible or praise and worship music on and let it play as you sleep. Sing songs of praises to God. If you are able to listen to music at work, listen to songs of praise and worship to God, songs that lift him up.

Teach the Word of God to your children. Let them know that they have a savior who loves and cares for them, and they can come to him with everything.

The more you read the Word, the more God will give you revelation of his Word. Your life will change forever.

Read: *John 8:36, Psalm 62:8, 1 John 1: 9, Psalm 32:5, John 3:16, Romans 10:9–10, James 4:8, John 12:32, Deuteronomy 11:18–21.*

Week 19

Study to shew thyself approved unto God, a workman that
needeth not to be ashamed, rightly dividing the word of truth.
—2 Timothy 2:15

Now that you have given your life to Christ and want to please
him more and more, you will have a desire for more of his word,
wanting more of him. Think of it like this, as you mature and grow
from an infant stage, drinking only milk (reading the Word), you
should move into the mature adult stage, eating meat (studying the
Word).

As born-again children of God, we must study the Word of
God. We should grow from reading the Word daily and move into a
time of studying the Word. You should still read the Word daily but
add unto it a time of study. Go before the Lord and ask him to show
and teach you how to study the Word, when to do it, what to study
and how long to study. He will do it. Now don't look at the The
Jones' and study how they study. Study how God gives you to study.
We are accountable for our own lives and are in different spiritual
places at different times in our lives.

During your study time, you should have your Bible, a Bible
concordance, Bible dictionary, notebook, pen, and paper. The concordance will give you insight as to what a scripture may mean, but
don't depend on that. Depend on the Holy Ghost to give you insight
into scripture. Only use the concordance as you are led by the Lord.

When the need arises in your life, the devil attacks you or someone needs prayer or counsel, you will say the right thing. Using the
right scripture at the right time, that is rightly dividing the word of
truth. If someone needs counsel or prayer for healing and you are
counseling and praying for finances, that is not rightly dividing the

word. As you study the Word and issues come up in your life and you need a word from the Lord, he will bring out what you have put in.

Study the Word!

Read: *1 Peter 2:2, 1 Corinthians 3:2, Hebrews 5:12–14, John 14:26, Matthew 5:6, 2 Timothy 3:16–17, Psalm 119:105, Joshua 1:8.*

Week 20

This is the day that the Lord hath made;
we will rejoice and be glad in it.
—Psalm 118:24

This should be a scripture that you confess every morning when you awake and throughout your day. When you confess this scripture replace the word *we* with the word *I*. Make this scripture personal, a part of your everyday arsenal to combat the plans of the enemy.

This scripture says to me, "Lord, no matter what comes my way today, I will rejoice. No matter what the enemy may try to do to stop my praise and trust in you, he will not succeed. Lord, this is your day. I will rejoice and be glad in it."

The Lord does not make mistakes. Every day he wakes you, it is another day for you to draw closer to him and give him praise. Another day he gives you to turn from sin and turn unto him to seek his face. Another day he gives you to pour out your heart to him. Another day to serve him with your whole heart. Another day he gives you to let him pour out his love on you, to show you that he is serious about his Word if you would just trust him.

Brian Courtney Wilson and Fred Hammond both have songs titled, "This Is the Day" (Wilson, 2015) (Hammond, 2006), based on this scripture. They are both good songs and will uplift your spirit. Listen to both of them when you get some time.

Praise him! Praise him! Praise him! This is the Lord's day, rejoice and be glad in it.

Read: *Luke 10:19, Philippians 4:4, James 4:8, 1 Chronicles 16:10, 2 Chronicles 7:14, Jeremiah 29:13, Isaiah 55:11, Psalm 5:11, Psalm 62:8, Psalm 122:1, Habakkuk 3:18, Matthew 5:12, 1 Thessalonians 5:16.*

Week 21

For the joy of the Lord is your strength
—Nehemiah 8:10

You find joy and strength in the Lord. When you feel as if you can't go on, when you feel as if you can't take another step, when you feel as if you want to give up, just think on the Lord, all the wonderful things he has already done in your life, all the promises he has made you, promises that has yet to be fulfilled. Confess those scriptures and trust God. Once you start to think on the goodness of the Lord, your heart will begin to be filled with joy. You will get strength to go one more day, to take one more step. You will get strength to keep pressing forward. You will get strength not to give up.

The joy of the Lord is "safety against enemies." It can inspire you, make you brave, and provoke you to serve God. "At all times, holy joy is a defense against evil. It imparts 'strength,' an inward power to do and endure the will of God. Joy overcomes temptation against discouragement and hopelessness in trying times. Joy protects against sin. It counterweighs the attractions of sinful pleasure" (The Pulpit Commentary, Volume 7, Ezra-Job).

Joy should always overflow in charity (The Pulpit Commentary, Volume 7, Ezra-Job). No matter how much you have, always give to those who are less fortunate. This really pleases God. There will always be someone who is less fortunate than you. Don't look down on them and pass judgement. If it hadn't been for the Lord, that could very well be you in the same predicament. And after you have given, don't look back on your giving and regret giving. Give with a cheerful heart. God will reward your giving.

The joy of the Lord is your strength.

Read: *2 Corinthians 12:9, Psalm 31, Philippians 4:8, Philippians 3:14, James 1:1–2, Galatians 5:22, 2 Corinthians 9:7, Matthew 26:11, Psalm 124.*

Week 22

I can do all things through Christ which strengtheneth me.
—Philippians 4:13

This is another scripture you should confess daily and walk in belief. It will not work if you just confess it. You also have to believe it. You must believe that Word of God will do just what he says it will do (Isaiah 55:11).

Christ will give you strength to do not some things but all things. He said he would never leave you nor forsake you (Deuteronomy 31:6), and he meant just that. It doesn't matter what kind of strength you need, mental strength, physical strength, emotional strength, it's in Christ.

It doesn't matter what you have to do on a daily basis, if you confess this scripture and believe it, you will be able to accomplish any tasks that comes your way. After all, it's not you doing it alone; you're doing it through Christ. He is the one who is giving you strength, strength to endure, strength to keep pressing, strength to keep your mouth closed when you want to give someone a piece of your mind, strength to resist temptation, strength to forgive others and mean it in your heart, and strength to walk in freedom and know that you are free.

You may have to confront someone and don't know what to say. Silently confess this scripture before you confront them and ask God to give you what to say and have his way in the conversation. He will do it. You may be tired at the end of your work day, and you want to spend quality time with your family. Confess this scripture and ask God for strength. Suddenly you're not tired anymore, and you'll have enough energy to spend hours with your family, forgetting that you were ever tired.

How do I know it works? Because I confess it daily, and God has never failed me. He gives me strength every time I ask him. No matter what the situation or what I need strength for, God is right there, supplying my need (Philippians 4:19).

Make this scripture a part of your daily confession and watch God do it.

Read: *Philippians 4:19, Romans 4:21, Matthew 21:22, Mark 11:22, Isaiah 55:11, Jeremiah 32:27, Deuteronomy 31:6.*

Week 23

Be careful for nothing; but in everything by prayer and supplication
with thanksgiving let your requests be made known unto
God. And the peace of God, which passeth all understanding,
shall keep your hearts and minds through Christ Jesus.
—Philippians 4:6–7

This scripture is saying to bring everything to God in prayer and supplication. According to *Merriam-Webster*, supplication means "to pray to God; to ask humbly and earnestly of; to ask for earnestly and humbly; to make a humble entreaty." So we are to pray to God humbly and earnestly, believing that he will answer our prayers.

God wants you to bring everything to him, not some things, everything. Whatever you have need of, bring it to God first. Don't do first, then when it doesn't work out like you want, bring it to God but bring it to God first. Ask him for his help in the matter. Ask God what you should do in a situation, then before he even answers, thank him for the outcome. Give him praise and adoration for what he is going to do in the situation. Don't have any thoughts or ideas on how you want him to answer. Don't bring to God what you want the outcome to be. Just bring the situation to him and wait for him to provide the answer. God wants you to trust him and to believe that he will answer your prayer, not answer in your time but answer in his time.

Once he provides the answer, don't complain or get upset with God if he didn't do what you wanted him to do. Thank him for his answer because you knew God had your best interest at heart. God is the only one (except for Jesus and the Holy Spirit) who can see down your road of life. He is the only one who knows what is going to happen, so trust him to lead you in the right direction. He won't fail you nor lead you astray.

You will know when you have truly given the situation to God because he will give you peace about it. You won't worry. You won't fret. You may even forget about it. Knowing the situation is in God's hand, and he will take care of it.

And don't try to fool God. Remember he knows your heart (1 Samuel 16:7) and knows if you are sincere. He knows everything about you.

Read: *Hebrews 11:6, Psalm 62:8, Proverbs 3:5–6, Isaiah 40:31, Psalm 34:1–4, Jeremiah 1:5.*

Week 24

Finally, brethren, whatsoever things are true, whatsoever things
are honest, whatsoever things are just, whatsoever things are pure,
whatsoever things are lovely, whatsoever things are of good report; if
there be any virtue, and if there be any praise, think on these things.
—Philippians 4:8

You must train your mind to think on the things listed in this
scripture. Things that are true, honest, just, pure, lovely, and of good
report. These are not suggestions from God but a commandment
from him. And if he commanded you to do it, then it is possible for
you to do it. Thinking on these things will keep you in perfect peace,
a peace that passes all understanding.

Now this is something you will have to train yourself to do,
and with the help of the Holy Ghost, you can do it. When you think
on the things God commanded you to think on, you will start to
feel better. Things will seem brighter. You will begin to have hope
and believe that you will win. That you are more than a conqueror
(Romans 8:37), and you can do all things through Christ which
strengthens you (Philippians 4:13). You will start to believe that God
loves you, and he wants you in his kingdom.

The enemy will fight you on every side when you start to take
control of your thought life. He will constantly try to disrupt your
thought process by projecting negative thoughts and images in your
mind. When this happens, you need to eject the thoughts immediately. You can do this by quoting 2 Corinthians 10:4–5. Then start
to think on pleasant things. Remember Jesus came that you may have
life and have it more abundantly (John 10:10). He came to destroy
the works of the devil (1 John 3:8).

Don't take a trip down memory lane. Before you know it, you will be back there. Thinking the opposite of what God commanded you to think—things that are not true, not honest, unjust, not pure, not lovely and of bad report. Things that will quickly bring you down and back to the past. The past is passed away; all things become new (2 Corinthians 5:17). You are now a new creature in Christ, so walk in the newness of life.

Take control of your thought life. Don't let your thoughts control you. Whatever a man "thinketh in his heart, so is he" (Proverbs 23:7).

Read: *Isaiah 26:3, Philippians 4:7, Jeremiah 29:11, 1 Peter 5:10, Isaiah 40:31, Romans 8:37, Philippians 4:13, John 3:16, John 10:10, 1 John 3:8, 2 Corinthians 5:17, Proverbs 23:7, Philippians 3:14.*

Week 25

Finally, my brethren, be strong in the Lord, and in the power of him might. Put on the whole armour of God, that ye may be able to stand against the wiles of the devil. For we wrestle not against flesh and blood, but against principalities, against powers, against the rulers of the darkness of this world, against spiritual wickedness in high places. Wherefore take unto you the whole armour of God, that ye may be able to withstand in the evil day, and having done all, to stand. Stand therefore, having your loins girt about with truth, and having on the breastplate of righteousness; And your feet shod with the preparation of the gospel of peace; Above all, taking the shield of faith, wherewith ye shall be able to quench all the fiery darts of the wicked. And take the helmet of salvation, and the sword of the Spirit, which is the word of God: Praying always with all prayer and supplication in the Spirit, and watching thereunto with all perseverance and supplication for all saints.

—Ephesians 6:10–18

Be strong in the Lord and in his power, not in your own strength and your own power to take care of situations but call on God and trust his power and his might. He is willing and able to handle any situation that you will encounter. I mean any situation. No matter how bad you think it is or how far gone you believe it to be, God can handle it.

Wiles is defined in *Merriam-Webster* as "a trick intended to ensnare or deceive; skill in outwitting; trickery; guile." You see the devil comes to trick you into believing the lie. He is very skillful at it and has had thousands of years to practice it. As a matter of fact, he is the father of lies. He invented them. He can't tell the truth nor does he desire to. He wants to do the opposite of everything God does.

Elder Woods, my husband, gave me an analogy of wrestling. You think of a wrestler. He is always moving, always planning, always trying to get the upper hand on his opponent, never resting. That's how it is with the devil. He is always moving, always attacking you, never resting, always trying to get the upper hand, trying to wear you out, never giving you a minute to rest. Just as soon as you finish giving God the praise and glory for taking care of one situation, immediately here comes another. This is where you need to stand. Stand in the armor of God no matter what the devil may bring at you.

All of the armor covers your front, not your back. This is so you will have to face the enemy head on, not cower from him and run. There is no retreat, nor surrender when you are dealing with the devil. You have to stand up to him face-to-face. Let him know that he gets no victory, that you are a child of God walking in God's authority. You will not be defeated. You will win. You have the victory in Jesus's name.

Don't be complacent with the devil. You are not fighting a physical battle but a spiritual one—one where you are fighting persons without bodies. The battle is not being fought in the natural (physical realm) but in the spiritual realm. You are a spiritual being in a physical body, so the enemy tries to destroy the real you, the spiritual you. You have to fight him where he lives. You have to fight with prayer, not arguing, fussing, and fighting. When you fight in the natural (the flesh), you are doing just what the devil wants you to do. Don't give in to him. When he attacks, go into prayer. And if you have a heavenly prayer language (praying in tongues), then use it. That will really confuse the enemy. He won't know what to do. What is going on. He will leave you alone, even if for a season.

You know how sometimes you can sleep and when you wake up, you are tired, and it seems as if you have been fighting all night. You have been! Dreams are in the spiritual realm, and that's where the enemy will attack. That's why it is so important to learn and confess scripture daily over you and your loved ones and rebuke the attacks of the enemy.

Confess Ephesians 6:10–18 daily. Make it personal. Put your name in the place of brethren. Use *I* in the place of *ye, we*. Use *my* in place of *your*. Walk in victory in the name of Jesus.

Victory is ours!

Read: *Ephesians 3:20–21, Hebrews 13:5, Deuteronomy 31:6, Isaiah 43:1–3, John 8:44, 1 Timothy 1:7, 1 Peter 5:8, James 4:7–8, Psalm 46:10.*

Week 26

This I say then, Walk in the Spirit, and ye shall not fulfil
the lust of the flesh... But the fruit of the Spirit is love,
joy, peace, longsuffering, gentleness, goodness, faith,
meekness, temperance: against such there is no law.
—Galatians 5:16, 22–23

Flesh is the unregenerate man focused on self, prone to sin and opposed to God (The Scofield Study Bible Commentary 2003). "The flesh lusteth against the Spirit and the Spirit against the flesh" (Galatians 5:17). They are constantly battling against one another. The one you feed the most will be the one that wins the battle. Please read Galatians 5:19–21 to see the works of the flesh and know that those who do the works of the flesh will not enter the kingdom of God.

But don't get discouraged. You cannot do it alone. In your flesh, there is no good thing (Romans 7:18), "but with God, all things are possible" (Matthew 19:26). Pray and ask God to help you overcome the works of the flesh. Dedicate your life to serving God. Purposing in your heart to cast out the works of the flesh and be filled with the works of the spirit. Be transformed by the renewing of your mind (Romans 12:2).

There is one spirit (the spirit of God) bearing many fruit. Thus, the "fruit of the spirit" and not the "fruits of the spirit." There is no law against this fruit. If you display them in your life, there is nothing God will say to turn you against them. In fact, he will encourage you to exhibit these fruit and put you in situations where you will have to use them.

These are the fruit you want to bear. You've heard it said, "You can tell a tree by the fruit it bears" or "An apple don't fall far from the tree." Well, you want people to tell that you are a child of God by bearing this fruit. You want people to know that you are from the tree of God, and you have not fallen far from Father God.

When you surrender your life to God, these fruit will become evident as he fills you with his word. As you yield to the Holy Ghost and allow God to take control of your life, he will push out the things of the flesh and fill you with the fruit of the spirit.

Read: *Galatians 5:16–26, Romans 7:15–25, Romans 8, Mark 9:23, Philippians 4:13, Romans 12:2, 1 John 2:15–17.*

Week 27

Order my steps in thy word: and let not any
iniquity have dominion over me.

—Psalm 119:133

Submit yourself under the mighty hand of God. Let him order your steps. Let him tell you which way to go, which way to move or to just stand still. When you submit to God, he will gently whisper in your ear and tell you which way to go, to the left or to the right (Isaiah 30:21). He is a loving God, and he wants to lead and guide your steps of life. He wants to bring you to him.

Submit yourself to God. "Resist the devil, and he will flee from you." That's what the Word says in James 4:7. When you are submitted to God, seeking his face, doing his will, the devil has no choice but to flee from you. Have a heart determined to do the will of the Lord, not to do your own will. Surrender to him. Let him takeover and lead you. Throw your hands up and give all to God. Say, "Lord I surrender all to you. I have tried to do it my way but my way does not work. Father you take over. You order my steps" (Psalm 119:133).

See won't God take over and work out some things in your life. *Trust him!* He knows what he is doing. He knows each of us intricately. He knows what is coming down your road of life. He knows just how much you can bear. He knows what, when, where, and how to order your steps. So when he says do, do it. When he says go, go. When he says pray, pray. When he says don't do, don't do it. Follow the leading of the Lord.

Merriam-Webster defines iniquity as "gross injustice, wickedness, a wicked act or thing, sin." Dominion is defined as "domain, law, supreme authority, sovereignty." Don't let sin have supreme authority in your life. You are a child of the King of kings and Lord of lords. He is the only sovereign authority. Don't let the things you have done wrong in the past determine your future. Repent, cast off the things of the past, and look to Jesus the author and finisher of your faith (Hebrews 12:2). The devil *is* a defeated foe. He does not have dominion over your life or anything that belongs to you.

"The steps of a good man are ordered by the Lord: and he delighteth in his way" (Psalm 37:23). Let the Lord delight in your life. Amen.

Read: *1 Peter 5:6, Isaiah 30:21, James 4:7, Proverbs 3:5–6, 1 Corinthians 10:13, Revelation 19:16, Deuteronomy 10:17, Psalm 146:3, Daniel 2:47, 1 Timothy 6:15, Philippians 3:1–14, Hebrews 12:2, Hebrews 2:14–18.*

Week 28

Enter into his gates with thanksgiving, and into his
courts with praise: be thankful unto him, and bless his
name. For the LORD is good; his mercy is everlasting;
and his truth endureth to all generations.

—Psalm 100:4–5

When we come before the Lord, we are to come before him with thanksgiving and praise on our lips and in our hearts. God loves it when you shower him with gifts of thanksgiving and praise. When you thank him for all the things he has done in your life, the little things, as well as the big. God loves it when you give him credit for *all* the things you know could not have happened if it wasn't for him. That money that showed up in your account right when you needed it, right when you didn't know what you were going to do or how you were going to pay that bill. The doctor's report that said all is well. You are fine. That car accident that you passed by two miles down the road. The one that you missed because God held you up a few minutes. Thank him and praise him for all of that. Because it was not an accident or a coincidence, it was God.

The more you shower him with thanksgiving and praise, the more he will incline his ear to you. He will show up. Now don't get me wrong, God is not a sugar daddy waiting for you to praise him so he can give you what you want. You must have a sincere heart toward him. When you come to him with thanksgiving and praise, he will give you what you need, although you may not think so at the time. He is a true and just God.

Make it a habit when you rise up every day and when you lie down at night to give God thanks. Thank him for everything he has done for you, even the trials that may come your way. You've heard it said that trials come to make you strong. I believe that. So when trials come into your life, don't get frustrated and ask God, "Why me? Why am I going through this?" Submit your heart to God and ask him to help you through. To give you what to do in the situation. I am a living testimony; he will do it.

The Bible is true. It has endured the test of time. It was true in the biblical days. It is true now, and it will be true until the end of time. The same God that the Israelites served in the biblical days is the same God we serve today, and it will be the same God future generation, your sons and daughters, will serve. The same miracles he was doing in the biblical days is the same God doing miracles today.

Grace is God giving you what you don't deserve. Mercy is God not giving you what you do deserve. Thank God for his *grace* and his *mercy!* Amen.

Read: *Psalm 116:1–2, Psalm 116:5, Numbers 23:19, Titus 1:2, Hebrews 6:18, Isaiah 55:11, Hebrews 13:8, Philippians 4:4.*

Week 29

Bless the LORD, O my soul: and all that is within me, bless his holy
name. Bless the LORD, O my soul, and forget not all his benefits:
Who forgiveth all thine iniquities; who healeth all thy diseases;
Who redeemeth thy life from destruction; who crowneth thee
with lovingkindness and tender mercies; Who satisfieth thy mouth
with good things; so that thy youth is renewed like the eagle's.
—Psalm 103:1–5

As I read these scriptures, the word that continually stands out to
me is *all*. All is mentioned approximately 5,621 times in the Bible.
Just doing pure math, that is about eighty-five times in each book of
the Bible.

According to *Merriam-Webster*, "all" has a few definitions. It
means "the whole amount, quantity, or extent of. As much as possible. Every member or individual component of. The whole number
or sum of. Every. Any whatever." Everybody. Everything. From these
definitions, you get the picture of what all means. It means *all*. Every
bit. Every drop. Nothing left out. God wants to be in control of *all*
of your life.

There is nothing that God and you can't handle. There is no situation that he brings before you that he will not give you the ability,
the knowledge, the wisdom, the strength to handle. It doesn't matter
what situation comes your way. With God, you are able to do it. You
must seek the face of God, ask him for help, and believe he will do
it. He will grant your request (Matthew 7:7–8, James 1:6). He will
give you mental strength, physical strength, spiritual strength, and
whatever else other strength you need to handle every situation in
your life.

It doesn't matter what is going on in your life, you must take the time to slow down and consult with God. Does that mean that you may have to get up a little earlier in the morning to spend time in prayer with God? Yes, it does. The Bible says, "Early will I seek thee" (Psalm 63:1). You must spend time talking to him and letting him talk to you. Letting him know what is planned for the day, then giving it to him. Ask him to help you deal with situations and people you may encounter during the day. When unexpected things happen during the day, take a minute and send a silent prayer to the Lord. Even if it's just, "Help, Jesus." I am fully persuaded that things don't always need to be taken care of right away. You don't need to fire back with a response to a situation right away. You can take some time, even if it's just one to two minutes and seek the Lord for an answer. God has shown me numerous times that some things don't require an answer right away. And even if they do, take the time and seek the Lord for help, then answer.

These scriptures are also praising the Lord. The writer is praising God with all that is within him. He is thanking God for all his benefits. He is thanking God for forgiving all his iniquities and healing all his diseases. With your spiritual mind, can you just see the writer standing before God? Sometimes kneeling, sometimes standing, with arms raised, tears streaming down his face. God loves it when we give him praise. The Bible says he inhabits the praises of his people (Psalm 22:3). If you have any sickness in your body, just imagine the Lord healing it. Imagine him healing the ailments, the aches, and the pains. You would be like the writer, praising God too. Now I am a firm believer in confession, and that you will have what you say (Mark 11:24). Psalm 103 is one of those scriptures that you should confess often.

What is it that you need to surrender to God? You see he deserves all of the glory, all of the honor, all of the praise, all of the worship, and he wants all your life, all of your problems, all your marriage, all your children, all your cares, all your concerns, all your hurt, all your pains, all your victories, all your defeats, all your job, all your health, and all your will. He wants it all, not just the parts you are willing to give up to him. He wants it all, not just the parts you think you can take care of. God is concerned about all of you, even the things you don't want to give to him, the things you haven't given up yet. He wants it all. Every little bit. From the top of your head unto the soul of your feet and everything in between, surrender *all* to him.

Read: *Proverbs 3:5–6, Romans 8:28, Philippians 4:13, Ephesians 3:20–21, Matthew 7:7–8, James 1:6, Psalm 63:1, Psalm 22:3, Mark 11:24, Psalm 27:4, Psalm 62:8, Philippians 4:19, Luke 10:19.*

Week 30

For as the heaven is high above the earth, so great is his mercy
toward them that fear him. As far as the east is from the west,
so far hath he removed our transgressions from us...For he
knoweth our frame; he remembereth that we are dust.
—Psalm 103:11–12, 14

God is merciful to those who fear him. Fear in this scripture is
talking about reverence to God. *Merriam-Webster* defines reverence
as "honor or respect felt or shown, profound adoring awed respect."
Mercy is God holding back what you do deserve. If you do a few
word replacements in this scripture, it would read something like
this, "So great is his holding back punishment to them who honor
or respect him."

You see it is a wonderful thing to honor and respect our God.
When you do, he is merciful unto you, not giving you the punishment that you deserve. You know the little things you say and figure
no one heard. God heard you, and you will have to give an account
for every idle word spoken (Matthew 12:36). The things you do that
are unpleasing to God, but you count it off, and you figure it don't
matter. That's just the way you are. It matters to God. He wants you
to have a renewed mind. He wants you always to keep him foremost
in your thoughts and do what will please him, not what will please
you.

When you confess your sins to God, he is faithful and just to
forgive them. He will cleanse you from all unrighteousness (1 John
1:9). He will throw your sins into the sea of forgetfulness, remem-
bering them no more (Hebrews 10:17). We are not perfect, and God
knows we are not perfect. He formed us from the dust of the ground.
When he formed Adam, he formed us. We are all seed of Adam.

Therefore, whatever Adam was, we are. God knows that, and he has mercy on us just like he had mercy on Adam.

Keep your heart to God. Seek his face daily. Ask him to order your steps, to show you what to do in *every* situation. When you mess up, as we often do, repent, turn to God, and ask for forgiveness. He is right there waiting and willing to forgive you and lead you in the right path.

Read: *Psalm 68:4, Psalm 71:1, Psalm 86:15, Psalm 95:6–7, Psalm 100, Psalm 103:1–5, Matthew 12:36–37, Romans 12:2, Philippians 4:6–8, Colossians 3:12–17, 2 Corinthians 5:17, Ephesians 4:23–24, 1 John 1:9, Jeremiah 29:13, Psalm 62:8, Psalm 119:133, 2 Chronicles 7:14, Acts 3:19.*

Week 31

He that dwelleth in the secret place of the most High shall abide
under the shadow of the Almighty. I will say of the LORD, He is
my refuge and my fortress: my God; in him will I trust. Surely
he shall deliver thee from the snare of the fowler, and from the
noisome pestilence. He shall cover thee with his feathers, and
under his wings shalt thou trust: his truth shall be thy shield and
buckler. Thou shalt not be afraid for the terror by night; nor for
the arrow that flieth by day; Nor for the pestilence that walketh
in darkness; nor for the destruction that wasteth at noonday.
A thousand shall fall at thy side, and ten thousand at thy right
hand; but it shall not come nigh thee. Only with thine eyes shalt
thou behold and see the reward of the wicked. Because thou hast
made the LORD, which is my refuge, even the most high, thy
habitation; There shall no evil befall thee, neither shall any plague
come nigh thy dwelling. For he shall give his angels charge over
thee, to keep thee in all thy ways. They shall bear thee up in their
hands, lest thou dash thy foot against a stone. Thou shalt tread
upon the lion and adder: the young lion and the dragon shalt
thou trample under feet. Because he hath set his love upon me,
therefore will I deliver him: I will set him on high, because he hath
known my name. He shall call upon me, and I will answer him: I
will be with him in trouble; I will deliver him, and honour him.
With long life will I satisfy him, and shew him my salvation.

—Psalm 91

This is a prayer of protection for you and your entire family. This
prayer should be prayed over your family every day, at least once a
day. It doesn't matter if your family members live with you or not,
even if they are in the same city or state. This prayer will keep your

family covered from the attacks of the enemy. Make it personal. Replace the thees and thous with I, my, me, and mine. Call upon the Lord. Entreat him for protection for your entire family.

Before your children leave for school in the morning, take a few minutes to gather with them and confess this scripture over them. While you are driving to work, confess this scripture. Expect God to do what he says in his Word he will do (Isaiah 55:11). Believe the words of this Psalm. Don't just recite it, confess it. Believe that God will grant your request.

Take time to read every sentence carefully and soak in what this prayer is saying. It is putting full trust in God. Expecting, knowing, trusting that he will keep you and your family.

From this day forward, make it a daily part of your confessions. Just like when you go to the doctor and he gives you a prescription and tells you to take it every day, this is the Doctor of doctor's prescription. Confess it every day.

Read: *Psalm 91 daily.*

Week 32

The LORD is my shepherd; I shall not want. He maketh me to lie down in green pastures: he leadeth me beside the still waters. He restoreth my soul: He leadeth me in the paths of righteousness for his name's sake. Yea, though I walk through the valley of the shadow of death, I will fear no evil: for thou art with me; thy rod and thy staff they comfort me. Thou preparest a table before me in the presence of mine enemies: thou anointest my head with oil; my cup runneth over. Surely goodness and mercy shall follow me all the days of my life: and I will dwell in the house of the LORD forever.

—Psalm 23

The Lord is your help and protector. He will lead and guide you if you are willing to surrender your life to him. Just like a shepherd leads and guides his sheep, when you totally surrender your life to God, he will lead and guide you.

You may have seen movies or even actually seen a shepherd leading and guiding his sheep. Wherever he leads them, they will follow. When he stop, they stop. When he go, they go. They are totally dependent on the shepherd to provide everything for them. That's how it should be with God. We should be totally dependent on him to lead, guide, discipline, and protect us as we move through life. God wants you to be totally dependent on him. He wants to be your shepherd. Surrender all to him.

Below is a poem from one of my friends in Germany. I pray it blesses you as it has blessed me.

Psalm 23
Author Unknown

The Lord is my Shepherd = That's Relationship!

I shall not want = That's Supply!

He maketh me to lie down in green pastures = That's Rest!

He leadeth me beside the still waters = That's Refreshment!

He restoreth my soul = That's Healing!

He leadeth me in the paths of righteousness = That's Guidance!

For Him name sake = That's Purpose!

Yea, though I walk through the valley of the shadow of death = That's Testing!

I will fear no evil = That's Protection!

For Thou art with me = That's Faithfulness!

Thy rod and Thy staff they comfort me = That's Discipline!

Thou preparest a table before me in the presence of mine enemies = That's Hope!

Thou annointest my head with oil = That's Consecration!

My cup runneth over = That's Abundance!

Surely goodness and mercy shall follow me all the days of my life = That's Blessing!

And I will dwell in the house of the Lord = That's Security!

Forever = That's Eternity!

Read: *John 10:27–29, Matthew 18:12–14, Psalm 46, Isaiah 30:21, Proverbs 3:11–12, Hebrews 12:5–12.*

Week 33

Trust in the LORD with all thine heart; and lean
not unto thine own understanding. In all thy ways
acknowledge him, and he shall direct thy paths.
—Proverbs 3:5–6

We must learn to trust God with our lives. No matter what is
going on in your life trust and believe God with all your heart that
he loves you. He has forgiven you. He has your best interest at heart.

Do not lean on your own understanding. In other words, don't
do what you think is right. Ask the Lord what to do and do what he
says. Because what he says, you know is right. He will never lead you
astray.

Sometimes we have to get into a quiet place in silence and sit
before God. We have to pour our heart out to him (Psalm 62:8). Be
cleansed from the inside out. Pour out all to him. Let him know all
that is going on in our lives, all that we need, all that we are believing
him for. Repent and ask him to forgive us of past sins. Ask for his
direction in our lives. Once you empty yourself out, wait on him to
provide direction. Don't move unless the Lord says to move.

We have become a microwave society and feel as if we need an
answer to our prayers immediately, but there are times when we have
to wait on God. Sometimes he says no. When this happens, don't get
discouraged. Continue trusting in the Lord. Maybe there is something you need to learn in the waiting. Maybe there is something
God is shielding you from when he says no, and maybe it could be
that God wants to show you that he is still in control and you can
trust him. Then he shows up in the nick of time in the waiting. It
may be in the nick of time for you, but it was always his plan. *Trust
God. He knows exactly what he is doing.*

Acknowledge God in everything you do. When you wake up in the morning, greet him with songs and prayers of praise and worship and invite him into your day. Ask him to take control of your day and give you the knowledge, wisdom, and ability to accomplish any task you face. As you go through the day, thank him for the little things like providing you a job, making it to work on time, making it to work without an accident, being able to solve a small problem. Before you go to bed at night, thank God for all he has done for you throughout the day. When you awake the next morning, start all over again. Make this a daily habit. The more you do this, the more he will direct your path. Keep your mind focused on him. He is the mark.

Read: *Hebrews 13:4, Deuteronomy 31:8, Psalm 62:8, Jeremiah 29:11, Isaiah 40:31, Deuteronomy 8:18, John 15:5, Philippians 4:8, Philippians 4:13, Isaiah 26:3–4, Hebrews 12:2, Exodus 20:3, Philippians 3:13–14.*

Week 34

But they that wait upon the LORD shall renew their strength;
they shall mount up with wings as eagles; they shall run,
and not be weary; and they shall walk, and not faint.
—Isaiah 40:31

No matter what decision you need to make take it to God and wait for his answer. I know sometimes waiting may be rough, and you feel as though you're going to explode. Things may seem to be getting worse while you wait. Trust God. He has you and the situation in his hands. He knows you, and he knows how much you can bear. He loves you too much to give you more than you can bear. After all, he wants you to be a witness for him, showing and telling the world how great and marvelous he is, not witnessing by what you heard but witnessing by what you've experienced. Waiting on God is the best thing you could ever do. Trust me, the best place to be is in the will of God. Wait on him.

No matter what you are going through, take it to the Lord in prayer. Wait for his direction. Wait for his timing. You will begin to get a renewal in your strength. You will begin to feel as if you can make it. You will feel as if you can keep going, one day, one step at a time. Hope will spring up in your spirit. When that happens, start confessing the Word of God over your life. Say what the Lord has said.

While you are praying and waiting, God will begin to work things out. You will begin to see him moving in your situation. Before you know it, he will have it all worked out for your good and for his glory. You won't be able to say anything but look what the Lord has done, then give him thanksgiving, praise, honor, and glory. He deserves it *all!*

Learn to wait and trust God. He will give you strength to run this race of life and not get weary. He will give you strength to walk and not faint.

Wait on God. Try him at his word. See won't he do it.

Read: *1 Corinthians 10:13, 2 Peter 2:9, Psalm 37:3–7, Proverbs 3:5–6, Hosea 12:6, Psalm 25:5, Psalm 27:14, Psalm 123:2, Galatians 6:9, Isaiah 55:11.*

Week 35

For God hath not given us the spirit of fear; but of
power, and of love, and of a sound mind.

—2 Timothy 1:7

Whenever fear tries to grip your heart, confess this scripture and 2 Corinthians 10:4–5. You will begin to feel peace and the presence of God. Fear will leave you, and you will begin to be strengthened in your heart, your mind, and your will to keep moving forward for Jesus.

The devil wants you to think that he has control over you, but he does not. He wants you to look at the negative things going on in the world and get fearful. He wants you to question God. No matter what is going on in the world, God is still in control! He is still on the throne!

The devil wants to keep you locked up in your own world, only thinking and praying for yourself, not witnessing and sharing the gospel with anyone for fear they may reject you or turn you in to the authorities. *The devil is a liar!* When the Lord puts something on your heart and on your mind to say or do, do it. You won't be alone. He will be right there with you. He will put in your mouth what to say and give you what to do. Trust God. He won't let you down.

The devil wants to keep you looking back at your past and fearful that you will make the same mistake, that you will slide back. He will have you thinking that no one loves you, so you may as well go ahead. He will keep bringing negative thoughts to your mind, thereby keeping you feeling sorry for yourself and having a pity party. When that happens, gird up your loins (Ephesians 6:14)! Stay focused on Jesus (Hebrews 12:2)! Confess the Word of God (Romans 10:8)! Cast those thoughts out of your mind (2 Corinthians 10:5)!

Start singing and listening to songs of praise and worship (Hebrews 13:15). Submit yourself to God, resist the devil, and he will flee (James 4:7).

Teach this scripture to your little ones. When the enemy attacks them, teach them to pray this scripture. The devil is after our little ones. They are our future. God has given you power over all power of the enemy (Luke 10:19). That power is the Word of God. Use it to defeat the enemy. God loves you. He loved you first. Yes, even while you were living in sin, he loved you (Romans 5:8). He loves you so much that he sent his son to die for you and reconcile you back to him (John 3:16). God has given you a sound mind (2 Timothy 1:7), a mind to make the right decision at the right time, a mind that is stayed on him (Isaiah 26:3).

I've heard it said that *fear* is *false evidence appearing real*. Don't be afraid of the devil. He is just roaring, seeing if you can be devoured (1 Peter 5:8).

Read: *Philippians 4:13, Psalm 118:6, John 10:10, Luke 10:19, Philippians 3:8, 2 Corinthians 10:4–5, James 4:7–8, John 15:13, John 3:16–17, Jeremiah 3:14, Proverbs 3:5–6, Deuteronomy 31:6, Hebrews 12:2.*

Week 36

Is anything too hard for the LORD?

—Genesis 18:14

This is a question the Lord asked Abraham and Sarah after he had told Abraham that Sarah would have a son. Now Abraham and Sarah were both old, and Sarah was past the age of childbearing. In fact, Abraham was one hundred years old, and Sarah was ninety years old when Isaac was born. Just like the Lord said, according to the time of life when he returned, Sarah would have a son. He returned, and Sarah had a son (Genesis 17).

When the Lord decrees a thing, it will come to pass. It doesn't matter the age, the color, or whatever shape it may be in. Whatever the Lord decrees will come to pass. If God has made you a promise, you have something to hope for, something to look forward to. There should be an excitement in your spirit as you wait on the Lord to fulfill the Word.

The promises in the Bible are God's word to you, those who confess Jesus as Lord and Savior of their lives. You should search the scriptures, read, and confess the promises and wait for them to manifest in your life. Don't get tired, don't get weary, and don't give up on God. Wait on his promises, no matter how long it takes. There is nothing the Lord will not do for you.

Your salvation is not too hard for the Lord. Your healing is not too hard for the Lord. Your forgiveness is not too hard for the Lord. The salvation of your children is not too hard for the Lord. Providing your every need is not too hard for the Lord. *There is nothing too hard for the lord!* (Ephesians 3:20).

So I encourage you to hold on to God's promises and his word. If he has said something to you, you can believe it will come to pass.

It doesn't matter how long it takes. It doesn't matter what he said to you. If he said it, it's done. You don't have to wonder if what God said is going to happen. You believe that what God said is going to happen. Wait for the manifestation; it will come in his time.

Read: *Genesis 18:10–13, Numbers 23:19, 2 Corinthians 1:20, Isaiah 40:31, Proverbs 3:5–6, Philippians 4:19, Isaiah 55:11, Joshua 21:45, Luke 1:37, Matthew 24:35.*

Week 37

But he was wounded for our transgressions, he was
bruised for our iniquities: the chastisement of our peace
was upon him; and with his stripes we are healed.
—Isaiah 53:5

This scripture speaks of the healing that was bestowed upon us because of Jesus's suffering on the cross. In the Old Testament, Isaiah 53:5, this scripture is pointing to Jesus on the cross being bruised and broken for our healing (present and future). In 1 Peter 2:24 in the New Testament, it is pointing back to Jesus on the cross being bruised and broken for our healing (past). Notice the use of the word *are* in the Old Testament (Isaiah 53:5) and *were* in the New Testament (1 Peter 2:24). So you see, it doesn't matter if it is Old or New Testament, it is pointing to Jesus on the cross being wounded, bruised, and punished for our healing.

You must have faith to believe God for your healing. You can't think you are healed. You can't wish you are healed. You have to believe you are healed. Confess Isaiah 53:5 and 1 Peter 2:24 as often as you need to. Get it down in your spirit. So when sickness tries to come upon you, the Word will flow out of you freely.

You may believe God for healing but still have symptoms. Just keep believing. Keep trusting. Keep confessing the Word of God. Thank him in advance for your healing. Then one day, you'll notice that you don't have that sickness anymore. The symptoms are gone. You'll get a report from the doctor that you are healed. Thank God, give him the praise, the honor, and the glory.

Don't claim any sickness that has come upon you. The Bible says you will have what you say (Mark 11:23). So when you say my diabetes, my cold, my high blood pressure, my this and my that, you are claiming it and you are having what you say. Train yourself to say this cold, this diabetes, this high blood pressure, or don't say anything at all.

Grab a hold of your healing. Let the devil know he has no more hold over your life. Walk by faith and not by sight (2 Corinthians 5:7). Hold fast to the profession of your faith (Hebrews 10:23). When the devil tries to talk to you about sickness in your body, you have to talk back to him with the Word of God. Confess the healing scriptures. Search the Bible on scriptures that speak of healing and confess them. Find out in the Bible where Jesus healed people and confess that just like he healed them, he can heal you. There is nothing too hard for the Lord (Genesis 18:14). He is no respecter of person. The same God that healed them is the same God that can heal you.

All of the stripes (lashes) that Jesus endured represented healing for us. Believe it and receive it in Jesus's name.

Read: *Proverbs 3:5–6, Mark 11:23, Matthew 11:37, 2 Corinthians 5:7, Jeremiah 32:17, 2 Corinthians 5:21, Romans 2:11, Hebrews 13:8, Proverbs 6:2, Psalm 141:3, Luke 8:50, Mark 9:23, Psalm 147:3, 2 Kings 20:5, Exodus 15:26.*

Week 38

Heal me, O Lord, and I shall be healed; save me,
and I shall be saved: for thou art my praise.
—Jeremiah 17:14

When the Lord heals you, you are healed. There are no two ways about it. There is no doubting about it. No wondering about it. He doesn't do anything half way. There is nothing the devil or anyone else will be able to say to change the fact. You must believe that you are healed then walk in that belief. It doesn't matter what you feel like. When Isaiah spoke those words, "With his stripes, we are healed" (Isaiah 53:5), and when Peter said, "By whose stripes, ye were healed" (1 Peter 2:24), they meant just that. You don't have to think about it. You don't have to debate about it. Just believe the Word of God and walk in the healing that Jesus has already provided.

When the Lord saves you, you are saved. Confess Jesus as Lord and Savior of your life. Believe in your heart that God has raised Jesus from the dead (Romans 10:9). Repent of yours sins, turn from your wicked ways, and turn to Jesus (Zechariah 1:3). You can't just say it and keep on living like you have been living. There has to be some doing on your part. Don't be deceived by the devil. Don't let him tell you that you are good, and you don't have to change anything. You must do everything to turn from your wicked ways and turn to God. He will be there leading and guiding you along the way.

Kenneth Hagin said in his book, *Health Food Devotions*, that he adopted a motto from Smith Wigglesworth, "I'm not moved by what I see. I'm not moved by what I feel. I'm moved by what I believe" (Hagin 2007). Believe the Word of God.

We should praise God *every day*. Praise him for *everything*. Praise him for your healing. Praise him for your salvation. Praise him for being God. Praise him for his mercy. Praise him for his grace. Praise him for the good. Praise him for the bad. Let everything that hath breath praise the Lord. Praise ye the Lord (Psalm 150)!

Believe God for your healing. Believe God for your salvation. Give him the praise that he so rightfully deserves.

Read: *Isaiah 53:5, 1 Peter 2:24, Romans 10:9–10, 1 Samuel 16:7, Matthew 13:28, Psalm 150.*

Week 39

And the Lord shall deliver me from every evil work,
and will preserve me unto his heavenly kingdom:
to whom be glory for ever and ever. Amen.
—2 Timothy 4:18

Jesus is our deliverer. He died that we may be free. God gave his Son so that we would be reconciled back to him. When Jesus died on the cross, the works of the devil were finished (John 19:30). His blood paid for our freedom. Every evil work the devil may try to bring upon you or bring to you was defeated when Jesus died on the cross. He was buried and rose with *all* power.

If you listen for the voice of God and obey what he says, he will keep you from every evil work the devil has planned for you. There is nothing the devil can do to you that will prosper (Isaiah 54:17). There will be no temptation that can come upon you that God has not already made a way for you to escape (1 Corinthians 1:13).

When you belong to God and something is not right, you will know it. You will get a stirring in your spirit. You may even say, "Something don't feel right. Something is going on. I don't know what it is, but something ain't right." That is your inner man, the Holy Spirit talking to you. Immediately put on the brakes. Seek an answer from the Lord.

If you say something, see something or hear something that is not of God, it should register in your spirit immediately. When that happens, talk to God. Ask for his guidance on what you should do or what you should say. If you react too quickly (respond in the flesh), the Lord will let you know. When that happens, repent, ask God for forgiveness and what you should do (if anything) to fix what you have wronged. Humble yourself (1 Peter 5:6) and be obedient to his instructions (1 Samuel 15:22).

God loves you, and he wants to keep you from every evil work the enemy has planned for you, but he won't do it against your will. Surrender your will to the will of the Father and walk daily in victory.

Read: *Isaiah 26:3, 1 Corinthians 10:13, Isaiah 54:17, Genesis 50:20, Psalm 46:1, Matthew 6:13, Galatians 5:1, James 4:10.*

Week 40

Behold, I give unto you power to tread on serpents
and scorpions, and over all the power of the enemy:
and nothing shall by any means hurt you.

—Luke 10:19

God has given us power over all the power of the enemy. This power is called Dunamis power. Dunamis is a Greek word that means "strength, power, or ability." It is the root word for "dynamite, dynamo, and dynamic" (Got Questions 2019), and we all know the power of dynamite.

Another power God has given us is Exousia power. This is a Greek word "translated as authority or power" (Got Questions 2019). God has given you authority over the power of the enemy.

God also gave us "the Holy Spirit, the third person of the Trinity" (Houdmann 2013). The power of the Holy Spirit is the power of God. Before Jesus ascended into heaven, he promised the Holy Spirit would come and be "a permanent guide, teacher, seal of salvation, and comforter for believers" (Houdmann 2013).

So you see, God has thoroughly equipped us and provided us everything we need to defeat the enemy. Nothing he can do will hurt us. God has given us dynamite, authority, the Word of God, and the Holy Spirit to combat every plan the enemy has set for our lives. There is nothing the devil can do to hurt you. He may roar and make you think he can hurt you. He may attack you with the spirit of fear and doubt. But he can do *nothing*.

Daily we are to seek the face of God and call on the Holy Spirt for help in every situation, when things are good and when things are bad. We are to keep our minds stayed on Jesus. He will keep us in perfect peace (Isaiah 26:3). So when the enemy comes, and he will, confess this scripture and James 4:7. Watch the devil flee. Nothing and I mean nothing the enemy can do will hurt you.

Daily put on the whole armor of God. Stay prepared for battle. "Fight the good fight of faith" (1 Timothy 6:12).

Read: *1 Peter 5:8, 2 Timothy 1:7, Mark 11:23, Matthew 11:21, Ephesians 6:10–18, Romans 16:10, James 4:7, Isaiah 26:3.*

Week 41

The thief cometh not, but for to steal, and to kill,
and to destroy: I am come that they might have life,
and that they might have it more abundantly
—John 10:10

The thief in this scripture is the devil. By deception, tricks, and lies, he comes to steal then kill and finally destroy *you*. Notice the progression from stealing, to killing, to finally destroying what he has stolen. The devil is not your friend. He has no good plans in mind for you. He does not care for you. He has nothing worth anything to give to you. He is a liar and the father of lies (John 8:44). Everything in you that represents God, he wants to totally destroy.

He comes to steal, kill, and destroy your happiness, your hope, your faith, your love, your joy, your peace, your mind, and your life. Everything that the Lord has given you, the devil wants to take from you. He will do this by any means necessary. He will use your family, your friends, your coworkers, your enemies, and even your own self. Yes, he will have you doing and saying things to destroy your own life.

Oh, but Jesus, he said he come that we might have life, and not just life but abundant life. He came and destroyed the works of the devil (1 John 3:8). Once you confess yours sins to God, repent of your sins, then accept Jesus as the Lord and Savior of your life and begin to follow him, then the abundance will begin to flow, not abundance in physical things like money, fame, fortune, cars, houses, boats, and the likes but abundance in spiritual things like grace, mercy, love, joy, peace, worship, praise, and forgiveness. Yes, he does provide physical things, but he wants you to seek him first.

Make up in your mind that you will not allow the devil to steal, kill, and destroy anything in your life. Make up your mind to seek God daily. Pray daily. Read the Word daily. Confess scriptures daily. Worship daily. Praise daily. Love God daily.

Live for God daily for the rest of your life and give the devil no place (Ephesians 4:27).

Read: *John 8:44, Matthew 13:28, 1 John 3:5–24, Matthew 6:33, Ephesians 4:27, Ephesians 6:11, Psalm 23, Psalm 34:8, Psalm 121, Psalm 150.*

Week 42

Come unto me, all ye that labour and are
heavy laden, and I will give you rest.
—Matthew 11:28

Jesus is inviting you to come unto him. He wants you to bring all to him. He is rest for the weary soul. As you live this life, you will go through trials and tribulations. Day after day, things will begin to wear on you, burden you. Things like money concerns, children concerns, health concerns, job concerns, and just everyday decisions. You may even feel a heaviness in your spirit and don't know why. I encourage you to go to the Lord in prayer.

Jesus doesn't want you to be burdened with the things of this world. He wants you to bring *all* to him. He wants you free from the tricks of the enemy. He wants you free to worship the Lord "in spirit and in truth" (John 4:24). He died so that you can be free. He is well able to handle any situation in your life.

It doesn't matter what is going on in your life, you must take the time to slow down and talk to God and let him talk to you. Does that mean that you may have to get up a little earlier in the morning to spend time in prayer with God? Does that mean you may have to spend some time in the evening in prayer to God? Yes, it does. The Bible says, "Early will I seek thee" (Psalm 63:1) and "Evening, and morning and at noon will I pray" (Psalm 55:17).

God is concerned about all your life, and he wants it all, not just the parts you are willing to give up to him. He wants it all, not just the parts you think you can take care of. God is concerned about all of you. Even the things you don't want to give to him and the things you haven't given up yet. He wants it all, every little bit from the top of your head unto the soul of your feet and everything in between.

He wants it all!

Read: *Matthew 11:29, Jeremiah 31:25, John 8:36, Ephesians 3:20, Luke 10:42, Isaiah 58:6, John 4:24, Psalm 62:8, Psalm 63:1, Psalm 55:17.*

Week 43

Greater is he that is in you, than he that is in the world.

—John 4:4

Prior to Jesus returning back to the Father, he told the disciples that he would pray to the Father, and he would give us another Comforter. That the Comforter would abide with us forever (John 14:16). That Comforter is the Holy Ghost or Holy Spirit as he is sometimes called. He is the third person of the Trinity. The first being the Father (God), the second the Son (Jesus) and the Holy Ghost.

Once you accept Jesus Christ as Lord and Savior of your life, the Holy Spirt comes to dwell within you. You are marked with the seal of the Father with the Holy Ghost. Once you receive the seal of the Father, the devil has no rights to you anymore. He has no rights to harass you, no rights to torment you, no rights to bring fear or confusion into your life.

The scripture says that the Comforter, the Holy Spirit, will bring all things that Jesus said to your remembrance (John 14:26). In order for this to happen, you have to know what Jesus said. What Jesus said is written in his Word, the Bible. So you need to read and study the Bible to know what Jesus said. When the enemy attacks you, the Holy Spirit will bring to your remembrance what the Bible said, and you will be able to fight with the Word. The Word of God is what will defeat the enemy.

You know how sometimes people may say, "something told me not to" or "something told me to." That something is the Holy Ghost trying to lead you the right way. When this happens, stop, listen, and obey what he is saying. He was sent by the Father, the God of the universe, to lead and guide you. Follow his leading. He will never lead you astray.

So when the enemy comes to attack you and wreak havoc in your life, just remember and you can even say out loud, greater is he (the Holy Ghost) that is in me than he (the devil) that is in the world (1 John 4:4). You don't have to wait until the enemy comes to attack you to confess this scripture, you can make it a part of your daily confession to encourage yourself in the Lord.

Read: *John 14:16, John 14:26, Matthew 28:19, Romans 5:51, 1 Corinthians 3:16, Acts 1:8, Acts 2:38, Ephesians 4:30, Mark 13:11, Proverbs 3:5–6, 1 Samuel 30:6.*

Week 44

Casting all your care upon him; for He cares for you.

—1 Peter 5:7

God invites you to cast all your cares upon him, not some of them but *all* of them. Anything that you care about in your life, he wants you to bring it to him. He is well able to handle it.

You may feel guilty by not bringing your cares to God, or you may think, "I just brought a lot of stuff to him a few minutes ago, and here I am bringing another bunch of stuff to him. I'll just take care of this myself, or I'll just wait and bring it tomorrow." Then tomorrow comes, and you forget. *No! Stop! The devil is a liar!* That is a trick from the enemy straight from the pit of hell. When God says bring all your cares to him, he meant just that. It doesn't matter what it is. It doesn't matter how many times you come before him. It doesn't matter if you have to sit before God all day and all night. He wants you to bring all to him. God wants you totally dependent on him. He wants it all. He doesn't want you trying to take care of your own life. He wants all of your concerns.

Just think about a baseball game. The players are out in the field with their gloves on, waiting to catch a ball as it is hit. That's how God is, standing with his glove on in the field of your life, waiting to catch everything that you bring to him. With your spiritual eye, can you see him standing there with his glove? Ready, waiting to receive everything that's hit to him. You can't hit too high, too low, too far to the left or right. He catches everything. I can just see him standing there waiting for the hit with a smile on his face, full of compassion, love, grace, and mercy for you, saying, "Daughter, I got that. Son, that one is out." Everything that is hit to him is caught.

As I said before, God doesn't want you to be burdened with the things of this world. He wants you to bring *all* to him (1 Peter 5:7). He wants you free from the tricks of the enemy (Ephesians 6:11). He wants you free to worship him in spirit and in truth (John 4:24). He sent his son so that you can be free (John 3:16). He is well able to handle any situation in your life (Ephesians 3:20).

Take some time and sit before God and just pour out your cares to him (Psalm 62:8). It doesn't matter how big or how small, just bring it to Him. Let him orchestrate your life. He said to me on 12 January 2019, "Keep your mind stayed on me" (Isaiah 26:3). "Stand still and watch me work" (Exodus 14:13). "The battle is not yours but mine" (2 Chronicles 20:15). I am a living testimony he will do just what he says (Isaiah 55:11).

Read: *Matthew 11:28, Numbers 13:30, Proverbs 3:5–6, Isaiah 59:1, Psalm 62:8, Psalm 103:14, Matthew 13:24–30, John 15:5, Isaiah 9:6.*

Week 45

Owe no man anything, but to love one another:

—Romans 13:8

I believe this scripture speaks of us being in debt to another. This is another trick of the enemy. He entices you to get credit cards and open revolving accounts. This satisfies that lust you have to buy what you want now and pay later. When later comes, you don't have the money to pay for the item(s). Then interest is added, and you owe more money. Over time, you end up paying back $10,000 versus the original $1,000 that you actually used. Now the money that should have been used, for the kingdom is given to the world.

Now lust is a work of the flesh, not of the spirit. James 1:15 says that "when lust hath conceived it bringeth forth sin and sin when it is finished bringeth forth death." The Bible instructs us to "walk in the Spirit, and ye will not fulfill the lust of the flesh" (Galatians 5:16).

God also doesn't want you borrowing money from any person. When you do, you become indebted to them (Proverbs 22:7). He wants you totally dependent on him to provide your every need, not your wants (pretty outfit, nails done, latest fashions, new iPhone) but your needs (rent, electricity, water, gas, food). When you borrow money from people with the promise (your word) to repay them, they are expecting you to repay them. Instead you stay away from them, avoid calling or seeing them, or you just totally distance yourself from them with the intent of not paying them or not paying them when you said you would pay them. This is not God's desire. His desire is that we love one another.

God is warning us to stay away from the trap of the enemy. Debt causes stress, anxiety, and worry (all from the enemy). Debt will cause you to work longer hours to make more money to pay off the debt. Then when the debt is paid, you are back in debt again. Starting the cycle over again. Staying in the cycle, just where the devil wants you.

I encourage you to get out of debt. Make a plan to get out of debt and be free from the grasp of the enemy. Go to God. Repent and seek his forgiveness for being disobedient to his word. Ask him to show you how to get out of debt and be free. He will answer your request and provide a way out. Once you are out, stay out.

Read: *Romans 6:16, John 13:34, Matthew 22:39, Proverbs 22:26, Matthew 6:12, Deuteronomy 2:3, Philippians 4:19, John 8:36, 1 Peter 4:8.*

Week 46

Hast not thou made an hedge about him, and about his house, and about all that he hath on every side? thou hast blessed the work of his hands, and his substance is increased in the land.

—Job 1:10

Ask God to place a hedge of protection around you and your family just like he did for Job and his family. The scripture says in Job 1:1 that Job was perfect, upright, feared God, and eschewed evil. This perfection is not being perfect without fault. There is only one perfect being, and that is Jesus. This perfection is being spiritually mature in the things of God. The way you get spiritually mature is to have a relationship with God by praying, fasting, reading and studying his word, meditating on his word, and just spending time with him. Yes, that means there are some things, people, places, and habits you will have to give up to get closer to God. The fear that is mentioned is not fear as if being scared of God but to reverentially trust God. Job had reverence for God. He respected and adored him, and he hated evil. Eschewed means to habitually avoid (*Merriam-Webster*). Job purposed in his heart to avoid evil, even the appearance of it (1 Thessalonians 5:22). He loved what God loved and hated what he hated.

In the book of Job, there is a dialogue between God and Satan. Satan did not ask for Job; God presented Job to Satan. Why? Because God knew Job. He knew Job would not forsake him. He knew that no matter what Satan put Job through that he would trust God. The only stipulation that God gave Satan is that he could not take Job's life (Job 2:6). Satan took everything from Job, his livestock, his servants, and his children. Through all of that, Job said, "Naked came I out of my mother's womb and naked shall I return thither: the Lord

SAVED, MADE FREE AND DELIVERED | 99

gave, and the Lord hath taken away; blessed be the name of the Lord" (Job 1:21).

You want to have the kind of relationship and walk with God where he will be able to say to Satan, "Have you considered my servant (insert your name)?" A relationship that no matter what goes on in your life that you hold on tight to God, not forsaking him, not blaming him, and not cursing him. So if you are going through hardship, it is not that you have done something wrong. Maybe God has said to Satan, "Have you considered my servant (insert your name)?"

Don't curse God. Don't focus on your problems or needs. Look on the needs of others and pray for them (Philippians 2:4). While you are taking care of their needs, God will take care of yours. And just like God placed a hedge of protection around Job and his family, he will do the same for you.

Read: *The book of Job, 1 Thessalonians 5:22, Philippians 2:4.*

Week 47

Submit yourselves therefore to God. Resist
the devil, and he will flee from you.

—James 4:7

W hen you submit yourself to God, you are submitted to his will, his way, and his plan for your life. You don't have any plans of your own. You don't have any say so as to where you go, what you do, or even where you live. No, when you are submitted to God, you go where he says to go, you do what he says to do, and you live where he says to live. It doesn't matter what the Lord says for you to do, you do it with gladness because you know it pleases him and you are being obedient to what he has said. I've heard it said that "the greatest place to be is in the will of God." I wholeheartedly agree.

The Lord will speak through the Holy Spirit with instructions on what to do. You may feel as if you don't have the strength or the courage to accomplish what God is asking you to do, but when you are submitted to God and has purposed in your heart to do what he says, he will give you everything you need to accomplish what he has given you to do.

To resist the devil, you need to be girded with the Word of God. When the enemy attacks you, you need to attack back with the Word. Once you realize what is happening, start confessing scriptures. If you can't remember scriptures, grab your Bible and start reading the scriptures you have highlighted. If you don't have any scriptures highlighted, go to the concordance in the back of your Bible and search your topic and go where it sends you. If your Bible is not handy, use your smartphone and search the Bible app or on Google. If you don't have a smartphone, just cry out to God, "Help." Oh, he will be there in an instant. Sometimes all you can say is "help."

God knows exactly what you need. Don't give in to the devil's wiles (tricks). Don't take a trip down memory lane. The devil is subtle. He knows how to smooth talk his way back into your mind and your thoughts.

When you resist the devil with the Word, he has no choice but to flee from you. Just like he fled from tempting Jesus on the mount, he will flee from you. Now don't get too comfortable and think that he is gone forever. He is only gone for a season. Standing back watching, waiting, seeking the opportune time to attack you again (Matthew 4).

Always stay girded with the Word of God so when the devil attacks, you will recognize the attack and instantly go into spiritual warfare.

Read: *1 Corinthians 6:19–20, Ephesians 6:14, Genesis 3:1, Psalm 121, Matthew 4:1–11, Luke 4:1–13, 1 Peter 5:8, Psalm 50:15, Mark 8:34–38.*

Week 48

No weapon that is formed against thee shall prosper; and
every tongue that shall rise against thee in judgment thou
shalt condemn. This is the heritage of the servants of the
LORD, and their righteousness is of me, saith the LORD.
—Isaiah 54:17

This scripture speaks of weapons that are formed by the enemy to
destroy your life to cause you to continue and eventually die in your
sin and miss eternity with the Father. Weapons like hate, unforgive-
ness, worry, stress, doubt, anxiety, debt, poverty, fear, fornication,
guilt, perverse thoughts, lying, vanity, rebellion and the likes.

Nothing the devil can conjure up against you will prosper.
Weapons may be formed. People may say and do things against you,
but if you belong to God, it will not prosper. There is no need to get
upset, no need to take matters in your own hand, no need to get on
social media and make post about the situation. Just bring the situation to God, and he will work it out. This will take trust in God on
your part and knowing he will work things out for your good and
for his glory.

You are made righteous by the blood of Jesus (Delgado 2013).
He and he alone died so that you could be redeemed back to God.
His blood paid the price for you to be in right standing with the
Father. It doesn't matter the accusations the devil makes against you.
Jesus is your advocate with the Father (1 John 2:1). As the devil
accuses, Jesus is right there saying, "Yes, Father, that is true, but my
blood paid for that."

If you belong to God, then this scripture is referring to you.
This is one of God's promises to his children and another scripture
you should confess daily. If you are not saved and walking with God,

I encourage you to give your life to God so you can claim his promises and enjoy all the blessings, forgiveness, and promises he has for his people.

May God bless you richly both now and forever as you claim his promises for your life.

Read: *John 10:10, Proverbs 3:5–6, Proverbs 62:8, Psalm 46:10, Revelation 12:10, Romans 10:9–10.*

Week 49

And I, if I be lifted up from the earth, will draw all men unto me.
—John 12:32

As people of God, we are to lift up the name of Jesus. Lift up Jesus who paid the price once and for all for your sins (1 Corinthians 6:20). Give him *all* the praise, *all* the honor, and *all* the glory for the things he has done in your life. How he died, was buried, and rose again with all power to redeem *you* back to God. How he saved you and set you free. How he delivered you from the hand of the enemy (Luke 1:71). How He forgave your sins (1 John 1:9) and cast them into the sea of forgetfulness. Never to remember again (Hebrews 10:17).

As we go through this life, we are to share with others what God has done in our lives. As you do this, people will come to see the faith you have in God and his Word. They will see the joy and happiness in your life, how God has changed you and set you free. They may even ask, "Why are you so happy?" That's when you can share with them the goodness of the Lord and lift him up. They may begin to think, "If he did it for them, he can do it for me. The joy and peace she has, I want to have." Let me caution you to be in prayer and ask the Lord what to share with people. Everyone can't handle your past mistakes, so be led by the Holy Ghost as to what to share. As you put your faith, trust, and confidence in God, he will give you what to say (Matthew 10:19). You don't know, the very thing you say to someone may be just the thing they need. God may use you to speak a word to them, and they respond by giving their life to Christ and start living in total freedom and victory.

We are not to lift ourselves up and draw people unto us. We are to lead people to Christ. Encourage them in the Word. Encourage them to read the Word, trust the Word, study the Word, and depend on the Word of God. God said he would not share his glory with anyone (Isaiah 42:8). So don't let pride puff you up. Stay humble before God. Always seeking his face. He won't let you down.

Lift up the name of Jesus. Let him use you to draw people to him.

Read: *Philippians 2:10–11, Revelation 12:11, Mark 16:15–16, Matthew 28:19–20, Romans 2:11, Isaiah 42:8, Luke 12:12, Exodus 4:12.*

Week 50

And he shall put a new song in my mouth, even praise unto our God: many shall see it, and fear, and shall trust in the Lord.

—Psalm 40:3

As you are listening for the voice of God, praising and worshipping him, he will sometimes subtlety whisper songs to you, songs that lift up Jesus, songs of praise, adoration, and worship. When this happens, write down the words of the song and continue to meditate on them. Sing the words and the melody over and over until they are in your heart, in your spirit.

This is a song I received from the Lord over a three-day period from March 26 to 28, 2018, entitled "Jesus."

Jesus

All the praise belongs to You
All the glory belongs to You
All the power in Your name
Jesus
I lift my voice to give You praise
I lift my hands to give You praise
I give my all to Your name
Jesus

Every day, you should have and sing songs of praise, adoration, worship, and thanks to our God. As you sing songs to God, he will smell the sweet aroma and come down to see who is lifting up his name (Psalm 22:3), who is sending up such a sweet-smelling aroma. As you sing, worship, and meditate on God, your problems will begin to just melt away. You will be strengthened to keep pressing toward God (Philippians 3:14). You will get energized in your spirit. Hope will spring forth, and God will respond with love and compassion.

Lift up the name of Jesus. He is worth your praise. Everybody praise (Psalm 150).

Read: *Exodus 15:1, Exodus 15:20–21, Numbers 2:9, 2 Chronicles 20:21–22, Psalm 22:3, Psalm 42:8, Psalm 47:1, Psalm 96:1–3, Psalm 138:5, Psalm 150, Ephesians 5:19, Colossians 3:16, John 14:6.*

Week 51

Now unto him that is able to do exceeding abundantly
above all that we ask or think, according to the power that
worketh in us, unto him be glory in the church by Christ
Jesus throughout all ages, world without end. Amen.
—Ephesians 3:20–21

God is able to do more than we can ever ask or think, but it is all dependent on your faith and trust in his Word and your ability to pray God's Word back to him. Put him in remembrance of his Word. Search the scriptures. Remind him of the promises he made to you as his child, then pray those words back to him. God honors his Word, and he loves it when his children remind him of what he said he would do, just like you and your children. When they remind you of something you said you would do, you get an extra push in your spirit. You may say, "That's right! Let me do what I said I would do," and you may even do a little more.

The Word of God says, "Eyes hath not seen, nor ear heard, neither have entered into the heart of man, the things which God hath prepared for them that love him" (2 Corinthians 2:9). Your mind can't even imagine the things that God has in store for you. Just think of the greatest thing that God could do for you. He can do exceedingly abundantly above that (Ephesians 3:20). He is a *great* God!

We must ask God and believe that he hears our prayers and will answer. Do not let fear, doubt, and unbelief shake your faith in God or his Word. He will do just what his Word says he will do (Isaiah 55:11). No matter how long it takes, you must persevere and stand on God's Word no matter what.

He will answer in his time, not yours. There are times when you pray to God, and before the words are finished coming out of your mouth, he has answered your prayer. Then there are other times when you pray, and it may take days, months, or even years for the prayer to be answered. Just trust God and know that he hears your prayers, and he will answer.

So if you are believing God for something, pray his Word to Him. Trust and believe that he will provide the answer. He will do exceedingly, abundantly above all that you ask or think (Ephesians 3:20).

Read: *Isaiah 55:11, Hebrews 11, 2 Corinthians 2:9, 2 Timothy 1:7, Numbers 23:9, 1 Timothy 2:12, Philippians 3:13–14, Philippians 4:6–8.*

Week 52

Being confident of this very thing, that he which hath begun a
good work in you will perform it until the day of Jesus Christ.
—Philippians 1:6

That good work is salvation. If you confess with your mouth the
Lord Jesus and believe in your heart that God has raised Him from
the dead, you shall be saved. With your heart, you believeth (continually believe) that you are made righteous by Jesus's death, burial,
and resurrection and with your mouth you confess it is, so you shall
be saved (Romans 10:9–10). Once you are saved, God will begin to
work out salvation in your life until Jesus's return.

God will begin to heal, deliver, make free, and restore. He will
set your life on a new path, the path he always had planned for you.
You must stay the course. Don't give up. Don't give in. Don't get
weary. Keep your eyes, your mind, your thoughts focused on Jesus
(Hebrews 12:2). Trust him with your life (Proverbs 3:5–6). Believe
and obey his Word. He knows what he is doing.

God will finish what he has started in your life (Philippians
1:6). It doesn't matter how long, stay the course with Jesus. The devil
will try to wear you out, one thing after another until you give up
on God. *The devil is a liar!* It doesn't matter what he says to you. It
doesn't matter what he may try to do to you. God has the final say,
and he is in control. Let me encourage you if you are feeling down,
hopeless, and just don't think you can take it anymore, call on the
Lord Jesus (Joel 2:32). He will be there in an instant. Encourage
yourself with scriptures and songs of praise and worship. You will
begin to feel better and get strength to keep going.

Keep pressing toward Jesus (Philippians 3:14).

Read: *Romans 10:9–10, 1 John 1:9, Psalm 34:4, Hebrews 12:2, Psalm 121, Deuteronomy 31:8, Proverbs 3:5–6, Galatians 6:9, Philippians 3:14, Philippians 4:8, 1 Thessalonians 5:17.*

References

Week 1

"Stop looking back! You're not going that way" (Author unknown).

Week 3

The Scofield Study Bible, King James Version. 2003. New York, New York; Oxford University Press.

Week 6

Merriam-Webster App. https://www.merriam-webster.com (accessed February 3, 2019).

Week 7

Preacher's Outline and Sermon Bible-Commentary, Wordsearch 12.

Week 10

"Believer's Bible Commentary: A Thorough, Yet Easy-to-Read Bible Commentary That Turns Complicated Theology into Practical Understanding," Wordsearch 12.

Week 12

Barnes' Notes on the New Testament, Wordsearch 12.
The 1599 Geneva Bible, Wordsearch 12.

Week 13

Sproul, R.C. *"A Simple Acrostic for Prayer: A.C.T.S."*, https://www.ligonier.org/blog/simple-acrostic-prayer/ (accessed May 1, 2020)

Week 16

Delgado, Iris. 2013. *Satan, You Can't Have My Promises: The Spiritual Warfare Guide to Reclaim What's Yours.* Lake Mary, Florida; Charisma House.
Merriam-Webster App, https://www.merriam-webster.com (accessed April 14, 2019).

Week 17

Through The Bible with J. Vernon McGee, Wordsearch 12.

Week 20

Hammond, Fred. This is the Day. Verity Records, 2006, Accessed October 06, 2020. https://www.youtube.com/watch?v=o5fXh oxJqQQ.
Wilson, Brian. This is the Day. Motown Gospel, 2015, Accessed October 06, 2020. https://www.youtube.com/watch?v=BwfN oBUtvwA.

Week 21

The Pulpit Commentary, Volume 7: Ezra-Job, Wordsearch 12.

Week 23

Merriam-Webster App. https://www.merriam-webster.com (accessed June 2, 2019).

Week 25

Merriam-Webster App. https://www.merriam-webster.com (accessed June 16, 2019).

Week 26

The Scofield Study Bible, King James Version. 2003. New York, New York; Oxford University Press.

Week 27

Merriam-Webster App. https://www.merriam-webster.com (accessed June 30, 2019).

Week 29

Merriam-Webster App. https://www.merriam-webster.com (accessed July 14, 2019).

Week 30

Merriam-Webster App. https://www.merriam-webster.com (accessed July 21, 2019).

Week 38

Hagin, Kenneth E. 2007. *Health Food Devotions*. Tulsa, Oklahoma, Faith Library Publications.

Week 40

Got Questions. What is the meaning of the Greek word *dunamis* in the Bible? https://www.gotquestions.org/dunamis-meaning.html (accessed September 29, 2019).

Got Questions. What is the meaning of exousia in the Bible? https://www.gotquestions.org/exousia-meaning.html (accessed September 29, 2019).

Houdmann, S. Michael. 2013. *Questions About the Holy Spirit.* Bloomington, Indiana; WestBow Press.

Week 46

Merriam-Webster App. https://www.merriam-webster.com (accessed November 10, 2019).

Week 48

Delgado, Iris. 2013. *Satan, You Can't Have My Promises: The Spiritual Warfare Guide to Reclaim What's Yours.* Lake Mary, Florida; Charisma House.

Bible References

Bible Gateway. https://www.biblegateway.com/quicksearch/?quick search=fasting&qs_version=KJV.

Scofield Study Bible, The. King James Version. New York, New York; Oxford University Press. 2003.

YouVersion Bible App

About the Author

Carmen Y. Woods is the oldest child of Jerry J. Rowland, Sr. and Ruby P. Rowland. She met Charles O. Woods Sr. in 1989, and they were married in 1992. Together they have seven children, Charles Jr., Essie, Sterling III, Reginald, Rashaud, Chandra, Courtney, and fourteen grandchildren. She is a native of Rockmart, Georgia and has seven brothers and sisters, Jerry Jr., Melissa, Tara, Lynn, Sterling, Micah, and Courtney.

She gave her life to Christ at an early age, and her desire is to see God's people saved, made free, delivered, and serving him with their whole heart. She is a veteran of the United States army, serving twenty-six years. Charles and Carmen currently reside in El Paso, Texas, where they serve as Elders of Restoration Community Church under Pastor Richard L. and First Lady Myra D. Dean.

CPSIA information can be obtained
at www.ICGtesting.com
Printed in the USA
BVHW031416180521
607630BV00005B/619